YOUR UNFINISHED BUSINESS

YOUR UNFINISHED BUSINESS

FIND GOD IN YOUR CIRCUMSTANCES
SERVE OTHERS IN THEIRS

BY

LEROY HURT

www.BookstandPublishing.com

Published by
Bookstand Publishing
Gilroy, CA 95020
2159_3

Cover design by Greg A. Bunker

ISBN 978-1-58909-438-3

Printed in the United States of America

ACKNOWLEDGEMENTS

According to conventional wisdom, authors should write what they know. Those with specific business knowledge would be strongest writing about business and those with extensive backgrounds in the humanities can succeed by writing about their area of knowledge. But how do authors learn how to distill the lessons of their experiences? I found my lessons in the influences of many in my own life.

First and foremost, God. Just as the Bible starts, "In the beginning, God…" my life starts and ends with You. I continue to be amazed You called me friend.

Without you Cathy, the rich experiences of this life would not have been worthwhile without my lady to share them with.

Kevin and Colleen, you taught me the art of fatherhood and improved on whatever good I could show you without picking up my bad habits.

Life may not have been fair to you, Brian, but you, more than anyone, have been my most important teacher. You show unconditional love and affection in spite of your disability, teaching me by your example to see others from God's perspective.

Mom and Dad, I'm sorry I can't hand this book to you in person, but know your work hasn't been in vain. Each day, I understand better the sacrifices you made to make life better for me. I hope when you look down here, you can feel proud.

Many thanks are due to those who read the manuscript and provided constructive comments, especially Grant McAllister, Matthew Boyce, and John Marlin. Any faults in the book are mine alone.

Leroy Hurt
Olympia, Washington

INTRODUCTION

Throughout a military career and in management and consulting positions in the public and private sectors, I wrestled with the challenge of integrating faith into daily activities. And in experiences ranging from deacon in a local church to delegate at international seminars about integrating Christian values into military professional ethics programs, the question of turning faith into concrete daily actions always came up as the central question. How do we live our faith in our families, our schools, our workplaces, and our communities? Can we learn how to do more than react to particular situations, hoping we made the right choice? Is there a way to understand how faith and daily living are knit together so we have a framework for making effective decisions? *Your Unfinished Business* explores how we can do that.

While writing this book, I often thought about the Roman centurion who sought help from Jesus Christ for his ailing servant. This man, responsible for one hundred Roman soldiers, certainly worked long hours, ensuring his soldiers were paid on time, were well trained in their profession, and were properly equipped for the missions given them by the Empire. In his years of campaigning, he probably developed a pragmatic and critical attitude. He was certainly pragmatic, the Biblical account crediting him with building a synagogue for the Jews in his geographic area of responsibility. This act suggested at the very least a practical sensitivity to the local culture and the need for occupying forces to be on good terms with the inhabitants.

And he could think critically. Having seen different cultures and encountered diverse philosophies and religions, he would certainly probe for authenticity, closely examining truth claims by others. So when he sent representatives to Jesus, seeking Jesus' help in healing an ailing servant, it's not surprising he told Jesus, "just say the word, and my servant will be healed. 'For I also am a man placed under authority, with soldiers under me; and I say to this one, "Go!" and he goes, and to another, "Come!" and he comes, and to my slave, "Do this!" and he does it" (Luke 7:7-8). He understood if Jesus were the real thing, there would be no need for the incantations and rituals he saw in the other cultures and religions he encountered.

Such incantations and rituals were designed to call down supernatural power, but if this Jesus were whom He claimed to be, He could heal the servant with a word. By giving such a command, Jesus, far from calling down supernatural power, would prove to be supernatural power itself. That centurion's background, therefore, prepared him to see Jesus for whom He was and act on that knowledge.

We're like that Roman centurion. Whether student, professional, homemaker, or tradesperson, we're faced with the same daily challenge of integrating faith with daily life. Like that centurion, we don't spend time pondering theory in an ivory tower or avoiding the world in a cloister. Instead, our circumstances daily call us to examine whether faith is truly showing up in daily living, and our backgrounds cause us to look for those answers with the same pragmatic and critical mind as that centurion.

So *Your Unfinished Business* is both a how-to and how-it-works book because we like to see how things work as well as do things ourselves. I'm fascinated with how stage magicians pull off their illusions and a number of successful books and Internet sites are devoted to explaining how things work. And large hardware stores owe their success to teaching customers how to do it themselves.

Because of that, the sections are highly structured so you can quickly see the logic behind the words. That structure allows presentation of a framework for understanding how faith and daily living can be successfully intertwined. You'll therefore find the concepts easy to remember and straightforward to apply. Small groups will find the structure helpful for supplementing group discussions.

Military and athletic metaphors appear throughout as well as references to movies. Military affairs and athletics deal with conflict, competition, and serious undertaking and are a common experience among people, so metaphors from military and athletic experience will help convey the ideas quickly. In fact, Paul the Apostle, the architect of much Christian thought, used those kinds of metaphors extensively in his own writing.

Movies are the cultural feature we moderns have in common and the stories they tell give us a common language. We know about "the force" and offers we can't refuse. And sometimes we explain a particular sacrifice by calling to mind how Bogie let Ingrid Bergman go in *Casablanca*. The common language of movies helps illustrate some of the ideas in this book.

I like to use acronyms because they help you remember the ideas you read here. That's important because recalling these ideas before they've become habits can be difficult. Using acronyms to remember the ideas will help you avoid those occasions when, some time after a particular situation, you clap your hand to your forehead and exclaim, "Why didn't I think of that then!?"

All verses from the Bible used in this book come from the New American Standard Bible (NASB). While there are many fine translations available, I've used the NASB for many years and have come to favor its words and rhythms for communicating the ancient ideas in modern English.

Table of Contents

1

YOU HAVE UNFINISHED BUSINESS

The red taillights of the cars on the gridlocked freeway during the evening rush hour commute reminded me of the television images of glowing lava flowing slowly from the volcano. At a distance, the distinctive red shapes of the lights seemed to merge into a glowing red river slowly snaking its way south from Seattle, channeled by the freeway's cold asphalt. But while volcanoes are evidence of change and renewal, the earth's crust heaving and shifting to create new environments for life, this red river epitomized the grinding sameness that swept dreams away.

"So this is the modern river of life," I thought as I gazed out the bus window, one of the millions rushing to and from work but not seeming to get anywhere. I too daydreamed about finding that ideal job that supported an idyllic quality of life but realized if it was out there, all of us millions on that freeway would have done it a long time ago. Instead, we all seemed at the mercy of circumstances we couldn't control. There must be a better way. And when I looked for that better way, I found it was with me all along.

That way is with you right now because you have something yet to do in this life. It doesn't involve finding security or success in this world because the alternatives fall short, be they spiritual guides, psychological thinkers, or gurus of financial independence. That's because they counsel you to resign yourself to your fate. Their message is this: You may not be able to control your circumstances, but you can control how you respond to them. If you're optimistic or have a positive mental attitude, these advisors say, adverse circumstances won't distract you from achieving your goals.

Nothing could be further from the truth. You *can* control your circumstances. Instead of fatalistically accepting what comes your way and trying to feel good about it, you can turn your circumstances, even the unpleasant ones, into tools that can change reality. You control your circumstances the way you control something entrusted to you. When you understand your relationship with the one who gives you something to care for, the sense of responsibility that orders your priorities, and the results expected from you, your circumstances will work for a greater good rather than work you over.

You may have been like me as a child, pleading with my parents to get a puppy. It's a familiar routine, the child pleading for a pet, the parents explaining the responsibility of caring for the animal, and the child promising to make the effort. Some children are true to their promises, but for many, the novelty wears off and realization of the effort sinks in. Some continue on, but a number fall away, and the parents become the ones caring for the pet's needs. We treat our circumstances the same way. Rather than taking up the challenge to do more than just react to our circumstances, we find it easier to settle for avoiding what's difficult and seeking what makes us happy.

But happiness isn't a goal to achieve nor is it a thing to possess. It's the byproduct of how we live. And how we live is determined by how we take responsibility for the circumstances we encounter in life. After reading accounts of concentration camp survivors and prisoners of war, one common characteristic caught my attention. They believed they had something left to do and pushed themselves to survive so they could do it. Some wanted to see their families again and others wanted to write a book. In other words, they believed they were responsible for something greater than their own comfort. If that attitude worked in those hard circumstances, it can work as a life principle.

The heart of that attitude is to stop expecting anything from this world and take up the unfinished business God presents you. Your unfinished business is to meet this world's needs for direction, decency, and compassion at the times and places God has placed you. He wants you to sow faith, hope, and love so others can reap truth, goodness, and mercy. *In other words, He wants you to become a steward of your unique circumstances, turning them into beacons drawing attention to the God who calls everyone to Himself.* This means your circumstances aren't benefits to enjoy or trials to endure. Rather, they're occasions coming to you as opportunities to point others to God or temptations to give up or go your own way. That's how you can control your circumstances – you control them by giving up control.

Stewardship of your circumstances therefore means realizing that who you are, what you know, and what you do are channels through which God touches this broken world. So stewardship isn't about money as it may seem in sermons you hear. Ultimately, pursuing your unfinished business, that is, being a steward of your unique circumstances, leads you to becoming a servant. And it's unfinished business because a servant's work is never done. Not only are there always needs to meet, there's always room for becoming a better servant. So how you act determines the outcome of your unfinished business.

There are several things to understand about your unfinished business.

- It's a burden for completing a mission that becomes a way of life.
- It changes who you are, what you know, and what you do from goals to tools. Instead of thinking about yourself as someone who has achieved a certain level of education or someone who is building a family and career, pursuing your unfinished business turns those circumstances in your life into channels for becoming God's friend, seeing from God's perspective, and becoming God's blessing to others.
- It therefore takes you in specific directions.
    - o Becoming God's friend isn't only a one time event; it includes becoming the kind of friend He wants you to

be, a deepening of your faith that helps you see God in your circumstances. And when you see God in your own circumstances, you realize He's in the circumstances of others as well, giving you common ground with those around you.

o Seeing God more clearly in your circumstances teaches you to step outside those circumstances and see from His perspective, a process of making His priorities your priorities. That's because taking on God's priorities expands your field of vision so you see Him in the circumstances of others, turning your faith into knowledge of what to do about it.

o And you do something about it because that knowledge becomes a burden moving you to action, a sense of urgency overflowing into activities that brand you as a servant. And taking up a servant's work is what turns you into God's blessing to others.

So pursuing your unfinished business is a life of turning what you believe into action, following Jesus Christ's example by integrating it into the intellectual, physical, spiritual, and social dimensions of your life so it shows up in your daily activities. But the remarkable thing about pursuing your unfinished business is you don't have be someone with great resources. Becoming a servant involves simply following the path along which God is directing you, not finding the right fit for you.

2

BECOME *GOD'S FRIEND*
TO DISCOVER YOUR UNFINISHED BUSINESS

How do you start pursuing your unfinished business? Saint Augustine said God made us for Himself, and we'll never rest until we rest in Him. It's easy to remember God in the hard times — we realize we're over our heads and beyond our capacities, so we look for help outside ourselves. However, the Bible points to full relationships like Enoch, an Old Testament figure who "walked with God" (Genesis 5:22). That means Enoch remembered God in all situations, the good as well as the bad. He didn't just run to God when he needed help, he became God's friend.

God makes you His friend to present you with your unfinished business, turning you into a new person different from what you were before. Not only does becoming God's friend uncover a desire to pursue the unfinished business He originally designed into you, the circumstances in your life develop you into the kind of friend He wants you to be.

This can seem threatening because change often seems threatening. We feel like we have to cast off into uncharted waters without navigation aids and without help. But this is what makes it so startling — it's not about changing you into something you've never been; it's about returning you to what you were *originally intended to be*. And what you were originally intended to be is God's friend.

God wants to make you His friend because He's actively involved in shaping your life. Some advice-givers acknowledge that God is interested in our well-being but refer to Him as Higher Force, Creator, Higher Intelligence, The Divine, or a number of other names as well as God. They want us to believe there's a benevolent higher power with minimal expectations such as exhibiting gratitude, demonstrating humility, and practicing tolerance and kindness.

These are nice virtues, but the God who wants to make you His friend isn't a one-size-fits-all God. He has specific and all-encompassing expectations of what a friend should be like that flow from His character. Some will say this God is hard to find because not all paths lead to Him. In fact, His expectations of what it means to be His friend are so great, there's only one path available.

How different is God from us? Superlatives don't mean much in a media-drenched society where those who would be famous strive to create outsized personalities to grab their fifteen minutes of fame. In a time when words like "most," "greatest," and "perfect" seem used up or worn out, how can we understand just how much greater God is? Here are some ways to think about it:

- Can you create something out of nothing? Through the wonders of nanotechnology, scientists can rearrange atomic particles to form new substances, creating material harder than steel but lighter than balsa wood. But they still need something to work with. Try as they might, they'll never be able to bring something out of void.

- Can you know the future? New ideas like chaos theory point out no matter how close you can get in predicting the outcomes of events, something can suddenly change without warning. In spite of extensive monitoring, we're still not sure about the weather and are taken by surprise when the stock market takes a sharp dip.

- Can you even know what's happening next door? A pleasant couple moved into the house across the street from my parents. They were quiet, polite, and kept up their property. Everyone liked them. Then the police and FBI came. That couple had been in hiding because they had committed armed robbery.

- Will you live forever? Despite advances in medicine, the best we can hope for is a shade over 100 years. But those latter years may not be very pleasant because of declining health and faculties. And future developments, while extending that life span, won't stave off death. No one gets out alive.
- And no one comes back either. A number of people have reported near-death experiences, but in the final analysis, they were never actually dead.

But God embodies those powers and abilities. An even greater difference is the quality of character God embodies and expects in His friends. It's that perfectly integrated combination of goodness, love, and truth we fall short of so many times. Think about these things:

- Even the best kind society is organized in a way that admits we can't measure up. A market economy is based on people pursuing self interest and a democratic government contains checks and balances because different groups in a nation pursue different agendas. The best we hope for is some kind of constructive compromise that benefits the greatest number of people.
- And that means some people lose out. But how much do we really care? At last count, average giving at church at any given time is only about two to three percent of reported income and overall philanthropy is only about two percent of the gross national product. So despite the vast increase in personal wealth over the last several decades and media coverage of billion dollar endowments, it's not enough to alleviate misery.
- We can't even meet the standards we set for ourselves. We like to say we live according to high standards, but how successful are we? Just think about how readily we put up unpleasant people. That is, we may claim we can accept people unconditionally, but are we willing to continually extend ourselves for their benefit? I just have to recall what I

sometimes say on a gridlocked freeway to know I can't do that.

But God is embodies all those qualities perfectly, creating a set of expectations of what it takes to please Him. So if you choose to acknowledge God as outside your ability to conceive Him, a God who transcends existence and experience as you know it but has very specific expectations about how you should live, then you've found *not the god you want but the God you need*.

Yet this God created you to be His friend. The writer of Genesis put it this way, "God created man in His own image, in the image of God He created him; male and female He created them" (Genesis 1:27). Those who become friends are drawn together by common characteristics, and being created in God's image means you have some things in common with God because He put them in you.

- It means you're a distinct personality. In other words, you're unique.
- It also means you have a distinct and infinite value. After God created the man and woman, He said it was good.
- Being a unique person with special value means you have a distinct role in the universe. You bring specific qualities to bear that no one else can.
- And you have a distinct way to fulfill that role. That is, you're a moral being, accountable for how you fulfill that role. It's no coincidence that God used the word "good" to describe how He fulfilled the role of creator during those seven days of creation.

That's what Saint Augustine meant when he said God made us for Himself. But that uniqueness creates a distinct need for communion because human uniqueness means that, unlike God, you're equipped for some things but not for others. That's why God made male and female — the two complemented each other's unique qualities.

And even more significantly, they had a direct relationship with God. Laterally with each other and vertically with God, the man and woman met needs and had needs met through their relationships. But when they decided to eat the fruit God forbade, they broke that relationship.

And we inherited that disruptive trait: we think by exerting our wills and governing our lives as we see fit, we'll be at our freest. It's like watching astronauts float about freely in their space craft, no longer bound by earth's gravity. They seem to be free, easily performing acrobatic tricks and effortlessly lifting heavy objects because they're unencumbered by earth's gravity.

But human bodies were made for gravity, and without compensating through exercise and activity, those astronauts' muscles would atrophy quickly. So, we'll never be truly free until we return to that relationship with God because that's how we were built. *And having that full relationship with God is the essence of His specific and all-encompassing expectations.*

Becoming God's friend is a process of being drawn out of your current life and into a new life in Jesus Christ. The change is so thorough you actually become "a new creature; the old things passed away; behold, new things have come" (II Corinthians 5:17). The choice of "creature" is significant: it suggests becoming something so different from what you were that you might as well be a new species.

It's also been described by the famous phrase "born again." Before you were conceived and born, you didn't have an existence. Coming into this world at birth, you start in innocence, full of potential and embodying your parents' hopes for the future. When Jesus used that phrase (John 3:3), He had that in mind — your change is so complete, it's as if your previous life had never happened.

But where the god we want isn't too demanding, the God we need is infinitely thorough, His expectations encompassing absolutely every facet of our lives. That's why you'll seem to be a new creature — God's expectations are so encompassing that aligning yourself to them means a completely new kind of existence. But because there are so many areas of our lives that have to be brought into total devotion to this God, *we can't do it on our own.*

It's hard enough to achieve whatever good outcomes we already desire. How consistent are we about diet and exercise? How long can husbands go before gazing at other women in real life or at Internet images of swimsuit models? How long can wives go before expecting their husbands to be the perfect men of romance novels? And do young people really mean it when they say "I hate you!" to their parents? Those may seem excusable in some people's eyes, but God expects us to be infinitely better than the best.

It was a never-ending source of frustration even for Paul, who complained, "the willing is present in me, but the doing of the good is not" (Romans 7:18). That's why God did it for us: we can't change course ourselves. We might be able to change for a moment but not for an hour or a lifetime. To rephrase Abraham Lincoln's statement, we can change a few areas of our lives permanently and all areas of our lives for a while, but we can't change all areas of our lives for good. And because we can't, we'll never be able to connect with God the way we were designed to do. But Jesus made it possible.

A gap exists between God and us because we're unable and unwilling to meet His expectations that flow from His character. In today's world of positive thinking, it's hard to imagine not being able to close gaps. We closed the gap between the earth and moon in 1969 when Neil Armstrong took his famous small step for a man, and we'll eventually close the gap between us and Mars. Modern transportation has closed the gap between continents, and modern information technology has closed the gap between time zones, allowing us to operate twenty-four hours a day, seven days a week, and 365 days a year.

But there's that gap between us and God. Have you ever gotten to a point where you realized you were absolutely helpless to do anything? My wife suffered a pulmonary embolism from which she eventually recovered. But when it struck her, those blood clots in her lungs felled her and there was nothing I could about it except watch her in pain as the hospital staff treated her, knowing any change in her condition could be fatal. I couldn't close the gap between sickness and health for her.

We can begin to understand the despair at recognizing there's nothing we can do to close the gap between God and us when we think about the despair that sinks in when we realize there's nothing we can do to help someone we love. It may be sudden and deep like those struck by Jonathan Edwards' sermon, "Sinners in the Hands of an Angry God," a sermon that helped ignite America's Great Awakening in the eighteenth century. Or it may be subtle, the steady drip of a life of wasted pursuit that finally reaches a tipping point.

And then it gets worse. Increase the intensity of that despair to an infinite amount and extend its duration an infinite length of time, and it approximates in a small way the outcome of never closing that gap. It will be the burning realization upon seeing God face to face that it will be the only time we see Him because after that moment, we'll leave His presence permanently and remain conscious of that absence forever.

So Jesus took the step to close that gap. The point of the Passion, the goal of the crucifixion, was to plunge into that gap and fill it so we could cross over to God. That shows how serious the gap is: it took Jesus' life to close it. He told those around Him, "I lay down My life" (John 10:17) to affirm His willingness to be the one to close the gap and also elaborated on how that gap would be closed, telling them, "no one comes to the Father but through Me" (John 14:6).

That's how badly God wanted to restore us to what we were meant to be: God was willing to let Jesus sacrifice Himself so we could become His friends. And that's also why Jesus

Christ is called Savior. Without His act of closing the gap, we would never be able to cross over, a fate from which He has saved us.

We can become God's friends the hard way or the better way. The hard way is by continuing to cross boundaries and drift off course until we get to the end of our rope and call for help. It can be a way of heartbreak, not just for us but also for those around us. In the New Testament, Saul of Tarsus was spectacularly transformed from being a vicious persecutor of Christians to Paul, a key player through whom Christianity expanded in the Roman Empire. But before his transformation, he was instrumental in the deaths of a number of Christians.

And a friend of mine left the gang to which he belonged as a youth shortly after he underwent such a transformation. But he, like others who came out of such lives when God transformed them, wondered what positive things he could have done had he not spent those years in a gang.

Yes, God can make us His friends by drawing us out of a wretched life, but it neither erases the effects nor eliminates the consequences of a life that was once adrift. For example, someone who came out of alcoholism still deals with the consequences of that condition and daily recommits himself or herself to staying sober. Although the example of such a life is a powerful and moving testimony to what God can do, the consequences of previous behavior linger.

The hard way, waiting until the situation gets desperate, can be very painful. The better way is to recognize the need to change now, embracing God early and taking up the unfinished business He presents well before reaching the end of our rope.

What you once saw *in* yourself and how you once looked *at* the world, you now see as unfinished business *for* yourself and *for* the world. That means God's friends can change the world because they can become examples that inspire others to seek God. They can do it because the work of pursuing their unfinished business makes their change and growth obvious to others. God's friends, therefore, no longer view their relationships as benefiting themselves or even others but as evidence of God's actions in changing them.

For example, slaves were enjoined to obey their masters because they no longer worked for their masters but for God, turning their labor into a tool to further God's purposes. Jesus even told His followers to love their enemies, a radical and challenging transformation of relationships upending how they looked at the world. So it's not that being God's friend has been tried and found wanting — it's that it can be found trying and not wanted.

Although God's friends behave differently, it isn't about reinvention or behavior change. Benjamin Franklin made a list of virtues he reviewed regularly to integrate them into his life. While that has benefits, it's not the same. Building virtues in our lives certainly improves our well-being, but we're still the same on the inside, just acting differently.

It isn't a panacea either. It doesn't fix problems: it's a starting point. If we think it's a "happily ever after" scenario, we may be surprised when "ever after" isn't that happy a time. Instead, it's being presented with your unfinished business and being placed in a position to pursue it.

Lieutenant General William K. Harrison began his life as God's friend that way, finding his unfinished business through his military service. His heart transformed into a servant's heart, he was content to perform his officer's duties as well as he could and allow his position as God's friend to be his motivation for excellence on the job. As he rose through the officer ranks during World War II and after, he purposed each time to leave his career progress in God's hands.

Each step prepared him for the next until he became the United Nations Command's Senior Delegate at the armistice talks at Panmunjom to conclude the fighting of the Korean War, putting him in position to lead the negotiations with the North Korean delegation. You won't always know for what you're being prepared, but you can be confident that God will prepare you for each step in pursuing your unfinished business.

Because becoming God's friend is an event that draws you into your unfinished business, it's not an easy thing that comes from reading a book or watching an instructional video. After redirecting you from your own dreams and aspirations and your deepest confidence in your capabilities, it starts the process of replacing them with qualities that make you effective in pursuing your unfinished business. You're emptied out and begin a process of being filled with something new. That something new comes from God.

But God doesn't leave you on your own. He brought you into this, so He'll see it through with you. Jesus assured His disciples that God would give them "another Helper" (John 14:16) to guide them after Jesus had left. This Helper is the Holy Spirit, and where Jesus was physically present with His disciples, the Holy Spirit is present in God's friends, providing the real time guidance and support that Jesus gave His disciples. It's through the Holy Spirit that you'll recognize the unfinished business God sets before you because the Holy Spirit is God's personal presence in you to help you pursue your unfinished business and guide you in your choices as you meet life's challenges.

So the choice before you is whether to become God's friend so you can take up your unfinished business. Choose to be God's friend by accepting Jesus' act of closing the gap between you and God and consciously committing to following Him. It's a simple matter of stopping where you are and taking that step. Dr. Francis S. Collins, director of the National Human Genome Research Institute and leader of the Human Genome Project to map and analyze human DNA, did that. An atheist, he began reading C.S. Lewis' *Mere Christianity*, acknowledged that God did exist, admitted there was a gap between him and God, and committed himself to follow Jesus Christ.

C.S. Lewis, too, was an atheist who made the same choice, capping years of reflection and refusal with a final commitment to Jesus Christ. And that heritage of commitment now stretches to you and invites you to join God's friends who have taken up their unfinished business.

3

CIRCUMSTANCES ARE YOUR **BOASTS** ABOUT BECOMING THE FRIEND GOD WANTS YOU TO BE

It's a truism that you can't be around grandparents very long before they start showing you photographs of their grandchildren. Boasting about things like that is a delightful diversion and reveals their pride in the newest generation. But pursuing your unfinished business gives you things to boast about as well. To refine the relationship you have with Him as His friend, God brings circumstances into your life to deepen those qualities He seeks in His friends, catalysts that help you grow and develop so you can pursue your unfinished business effectively.

That growing dependence on God instead of yourself is what you'll be able to boast about. For although God now regards you as His friend, He wants that friendship to achieve its potential. But it's your choice: your stewardship of the circumstances in your life determines your progress.

Your circumstances span the spectrum of human experience and make you aware you need more than just your own capabilities. Because we can know what others experience, circumstances can be a common language helping us communicate with others. Everyone is somewhere on that spectrum of experience and knowing an appropriate word to speak can plant a seed that will bear fruit at a later time. So God's presence in your circumstances can be something to boast about that's even greater than what those grandparents have.

Boasting means something different in the Bible, revolving around inadequacy for a given task. Biblical boasting means giving all credit to God so others can see Him in your circumstances. And when they can see God in your circumstances, they'll begin to look for Him in their own, a step toward their becoming God's friend themselves.

Jeremiah records God as saying, "Let not a wise man boast of his wisdom, and let not the mighty man boast of his might, let not a rich man boast of his riches; but let him who boasts boast of this, that he understands and knows Me" (Jeremiah 9:23,24). Biblical boasting, therefore, isn't a prideful act but simply *redirecting attention from yourself and your capabilities to God and His provision.*

The word, "boasting," then, is really a term chosen to illustrate the certainty and conviction with which you direct attention to God. This is in stark contrast to the ancient Greeks, Vikings, and other peoples for whom boasting meant highlighting their own accomplishments to ensure a measure of immortality.

And being able to boast about what God has done also shows a change in what you think is important because you're becoming the friend God wants you to be. So critical is your understanding of how God uses those circumstances that I developed an acronym to help you remember them. Because the end result is your being able to boast in what God has done for you, that acronym is BOASTS. What are some of those ways in which you can boast?

- *Blessings* let you boast about how God has taught you to do things His way
- *Opportunity* lets you boast about how God has awakened in you a desire to do things His way
- *Adversity* lets you boast about how God has delivered you through difficult circumstances
- *Suffering* lets you boast about how God has comforted you when you were afflicted by others
- *Temptation* lets you boast about how God rescued you from a desire to do things your way
- *Sin* lets you boast about how God restored you to a full relationship with Him even after you did things your way

Character beacons are what everyone desires

Everyone wants good things in their lives. In terms of your unfinished business, these good things are beacons that highlight what you're doing and draw others into your path. Sometimes called serendipity or providence, *blessings* and *opportunity* reveal you've learned your lessons and are ready for more responsibility. By broadcasting the quality of your character, they turn you into a beacon and allow God to give you a greater platform from which you can affect the world.

Blessings show you learned to do things God's way

I used to think of blessings as good things that came my way. Period. Instead, blessings are confirmation you learned to do things God's way and are being prepared and positioned for greater things. If you get promoted at work, it's not because God wants you to earn more and have more prestige; it's because He's entrusting greater responsibility to you and enlarging your mission. If an elite college accepts you, it's not because God is glorifying you for your great intelligence; it's because He expects you to train your mind for a greater purpose. Defined that way, *even unfavorable circumstances can become blessings* because they allow you to point to God as your support.

Blessings are possible because there's no such thing as "happily ever after" in this life. The lepers Jesus healed had to reintegrate themselves back into their communities and get on with life, an opportunity to be beacons where they lived. And the lame man whom the apostle Peter healed showed that blessings are for a greater purpose than benefiting the recipient. After Peter's healing words, the lame man "entered the temple with them, walking and leaping and praising God" (Acts 3:8). In other words, he was pointing to God as the source of his new condition, boasting to others about what God had done.

The world in which the writers of the Bible lived understood the requirement to do more with circumstances than just enjoy or complain about them. Successful Roman generals received a triumph when they returned to Rome, a parade that included captives and trophies from the lands they conquered and showed they had discharged their responsibilities effectively.

Having been given a good thing, their rank and scope of responsibility, they didn't sit back and enjoy the privileges of their station; instead, they fulfilled the mission given to them by Rome. So if those entrusted with benefits in this world understand the need to do something about those benefits, how much more those who have become God's friends and are entrusted with infinitely greater benefits?

In other words, you're blessed because you learned how to turn your circumstances into occasions for pointing others to God. When something good comes your way, it's not just to benefit you but also to give you a resource for meeting a need in the world. For example, Joseph received a significant benefit when he was elevated to his high position in Egypt just below Pharaoh. After a period of seemingly endless descent from the pit in which his brothers cast him to slavery in Egypt to a dungeon, Joseph began an amazing ascent in the Egyptian hierarchy because of his faithfulness.

Successfully interpreting Pharaoh's dream as a foretelling of seven years of plenty followed by seven years of famine, Joseph recommended a way to prepare for the famine years and was appointed prime minister by Pharaoh to put that recommendation into action. Each time, Joseph advanced farther in the Egyptian hierarchy, and each time he used that new position to meet a need. The blessing wasn't the new and greater position but his growth in using it to have greater impact.

So although given a larger responsibility after successfully interpreting Pharaoh's dream, Joseph didn't use that exalted position to enjoy himself; instead he obeyed Pharaoh by launching a program to prepare Egypt for the coming famine, saving lives and turning Egypt into a greater economic power as well as becoming the vehicle by which the rest of Joseph's family was saved from the famine and positioned to become the nation of Israel.

It works that way because blessings are character related. It's easy to think of blessings as benefits and leave it at that. But those circumstances are really resources given to you so you can have greater impact. Whether it's more time, better position, great talent, or more treasure, they make you more effective in pursuing your unfinished business. But the remarkable impact comes when you learn to be a steward of even unpleasant circumstances, a development of your character that's the blessing for you.

You may think of such stewardship in material terms and have a picture of famous philanthropists in your mind. Names like the Rockefeller Foundation and the Bill and Melinda Gates Foundation call to mind giving large amounts of money to charitable causes, and relief organizations like World Vision and Samaritan's Purse provide material relief directly to people. Material enlargement can certainly be an opportunity to turn your benefits into blessings by using a portion to meet needs God has shown you.

But blessings also exist in the spiritual realm. When I was ordained a deacon in a Southern Baptist church, I was given a benefit of recognition but was also charged to turn it into a blessing by using the new position to serve the congregation and help grow that church's ministry. Responsibilities included church administration, teaching, and example-setting.

The ceremony itself included a laying on of hands by the pastor and other deacons that evoked the stories of Old Testament patriarchs giving a blessing to their children and Biblical figures being anointed for specific tasks. It was a ceremony designed to stress the continuity of service and responsibilities of stewardship.

Blessings aren't an assurance of perfect health or greater wealth. That means you can still be afflicted with your version of Paul's thorn in the flesh. So what you receive is always a blessing but not always a benefit. I watched the movie *End of the Spear* about several missionaries killed by the tribe they were trying to reach. Their wives took their turn reaching out to that tribe, amazing the tribe's members because there was no desire for revenge, only love.

The tribe fully understood the common language of those circumstances and stepped into the light of God's friendship. But the slain missionaries, having set the stage for that tribe's conversion and turning away from a violence-ridden culture, didn't see the fruits of their stewardship in this world.

As successful stewardship of your circumstances, blessings enlarge God's impact in the world because He's chosen to affect the world through you. You therefore expand God's influence in the world by making His concern concrete. You're more than the messenger — you're the agent. In law, an agent is someone empowered to act for someone else.

When the military transferred me to another duty station, especially overseas, I sometimes had to leave my wife behind until I found a place to live. She stayed back and got our belongings packed up. I had to provide her with power of attorney so various agencies knew she had the authority to make decisions in my absence. Your stewardship of blessings God has given you put you in a position to be an agent and act on God's behalf.

Blessings are also a sign you're being positioned for stewardship of even larger circumstances. As you develop as a steward, you can begin to have a greater impact. That's because you have a chance to reflect on what you've done and devote yourself to building on your earlier work. It also allows you to turn into blessings what you once thought were setbacks. This is what James had in mind when he said, "Consider it all joy, my brethren, when you encounter various trials" (James 1:2). Being able to turn what others regard as setbacks into blessings expands your impact.

God's vision of your potential means He will expect much from you because "From everyone who has been given much, much will be required "(Luke 12:48). You can meet that expectation by committing ahead of time to be an effective steward of your circumstances. The Chick-Fil-A line of restaurants is known for not operating on Sundays, one of their founding principles being to honor God in their work. That policy draws attention from others and puts the firm in the position of being able to explain the basis of that policy.

Opportunity is a desire to do things God's way

Where blessings are your stewardship of turning circumstances God has given you into actions and outcomes that support His greater purposes, opportunity is the set of choices before you appealing to a desire to be such a steward. Before you act in a certain way, you have to choose to act in that way, selecting a course of action from among a number of options. The options before you to do things God's way constitute opportunity. These decisions can be nice problems to have: deciding which home to buy, which college offer to accept, or whether to propose marriage. David directs you to God's words as the source of wisdom in making those decisions, testifying, "Your word is a lamp to my feet And a light to my path" (Psalm 119:105).

Being presented with an opportunity means God has chosen you for a particular task but has given you control over whether you choose to do it. Dictionaries define opportunity as a favorable coming together of circumstances, making it an intersection between your present situation and future possibilities and giving you a number of options to choose from. It can range from life-changing decisions like what profession to choose to seemingly small decisions like which church to attend. Yet, what you finally choose affects how effectively you pursue your unfinished business.

Jesus' parable of the talents illustrates how opportunity appears in your life. Three servants were given a sum of money to manage and chose to do different things with it. Two used their amounts to turn a profit and one sat on his share and didn't get a return. All three had similar opportunities, but not all of them made wise decisions. Opportunity is the test of how well you've prepared. In a way, it's a tougher choice than how to respond to adversity or temptation because the possible outcomes often seem good enough to make you think you can't possibly lose.

So opportunity isn't a triumph or disaster because you haven't chosen. You have some options that can have varying effects. But because self-focused desires are never far away, temptation can come alongside to keep you from making the right choice when presented an opportunity. Temptation does that by trying to convince you that gratifying self-focused desires is how you can meet the particular need.

This all means opportunity is the path to blessings. You're presented with choices that can lead to specific outcomes if you choose wisely. The challenge in opportunity is being able to recognize it for what it is. Because the choice can result in favorable outcomes, opportunity hands you the ability to have a positive impact.

This can be harder than the choices temptation presents you because you feel a greater burden to choose that which would have the best outcome. After all, if you could do something that was good enough for someone or another thing that was the best for that person, wouldn't you want to choose what was best? The challenge is being able to tell the difference.

Preparation, therefore, is the key to being a steward of opportunity. A popular joke describes a tourist who wanted to visit Carnegie Hall. He saw someone carrying a case that obviously held a violin and surmised that person was a musician and could provide directions.

"Pardon me," the tourist asked, "But how do you get to Carnegie Hall?"

"Practice, practice, and more practice," replied the musician.

Preparation sets the stage for recognizing opportunities and includes awareness of situations around you because opportunities exist in unlikely places. King Solomon engaged in the critical component of preparation by seeking wisdom. When God told him he could have riches and power, Solomon asked instead for wisdom. And because Solomon asked for wisdom, God gave him wealth, fame, and power.

Character builders are everyone's lot

Everyone must endure *adversity* and *suffering*, life situations that build character if you let them. It's not enough to respond with a stiff upper lip — you must commit to letting God use those times to shape you in ways that improve your strength and endurance for your unfinished business.

Adversity and suffering open you to God's work in your life because they're when you're most likely to turn to God. They bring you to the end of your rope and push you to admit you're not in control. We may still think those situations aren't fair, but if God were truly fair and gave us what we deserved, who could stand?

They're like polishing glass and metal. The craftsman subjects the material to harsh treatments like heating and grinding to turn them into useful products. At the end, the materials reflect the image of whoever looks at them. That's the effect adversity and suffering have on your life. God, the master craftsman, wants to turn you into a polished vessel that reflects His image.

And there are some times when what you think are adversity or suffering are actually signals to slow down so you can recover from fatigue, a dangerous condition that can become sloth, one of the seven deadly sins. In Christian tradition, sloth was not just laziness but a malignant apathy or depression about spiritual matters.

That's because fatigue makes you think more about your own needs. It can come from experiencing too much suffering and adversity or even from trying to do too much. And the effect is to make you want to pull back from the effort, rationalizing that everyone needs a break. The great football coach, Vince Lombardi, characterized that effect, saying, "Fatigue makes cowards of us all."

Adversity happens to everyone

We all face hard times. A close relative died, someone was laid off, we feel anxious about the future. We want David's words to comfort us as they have comforted generations, expressing the assurance, "Even though I walk through the valley of the shadow of death, I fear no evil, for You are with me" (Psalm 23:4). Difficult circumstances can happen to anyone, but they become part of your unfinished business because you can demonstrate your confidence in God to others and God can use those situations for good.

Adversity comes your way because you live in a fallen world populated with fallen people. It's easy to overlook that fact when you're in the middle of difficult circumstances, but that simple fact means adversity is inevitable. You didn't ask for it, you probably didn't do anything to deserve it, and you certainly didn't go out of your way looking for it. Adversity finds you — you can run but you can't hide. It's important to remember that adversity isn't a result of your choices regarding your unfinished business or your faith.

Because you live in a fallen world, all circumstances are in a state of flux and life seems chaotic. There's enough unpredictability that Murphy's Law, the principle that things will go wrong at the worst possible time, is more than a humorous comment. Understanding that adversity is inevitable helps you realize some things just aren't your fault. You still have to prepare for and deal with those situations, but they're not something you can control.

You're therefore subject to the results of other people's choices as well as the vagaries of an imperfect world. If a drunk driver hits you while you're driving your car, it's because that driver made a decision to do something that impaired his or her ability to drive safely. And if a storm damages your house, it's because storms gather and create havoc. These incidents don't come about because of choices you made regarding your relationship with God. But it doesn't mean God won't use your experience to show you a higher purpose or use you to bless others.

Bonsai is a gardening art that produces beautiful plants that are miniature versions of the actual plants or trees. By keeping the plant in a pot to restrict its roots as well as pruning it, the gardener can create something that looks astonishingly like its larger version even though it's only about one-tenth the size. The character of Mr. Miyagi in the movie, *The Karate Kid*, conveyed the patience and deliberation required in creating these natural works of art. A snip here, a twist of the wire there, and the plant would eventually grow in the direction and shape the gardener intended.

In God's hands, adversity can be a shaping process much like bonsai, directing your growth so you develop the precise characteristics God wants. Jesus likened God's work in believers' lives to that of the vinedresser, for "every branch that bears fruit, He prunes it so that it may bear more fruit" (John 15:2). The pruning action sounds hard because it is. The more God prunes you, the more you understand your own inadequacy and the need to turn utterly to Him, the sign of maturity and readiness for ministry.

Subsequent adversity is the testing that validates what God has done. Ideally, you want to be effective in the face of adversity and even be able to help others through it. I used to joke that learning by experience means the test comes before the lesson. I now think it's not as much a joke as it is a truism — the effect of encountering the experience first makes the need for the lesson more urgent because my desire to make the discomfort stop makes me cast about for a solution. And when that solution isn't forthcoming, I turn to God, something He wants me to do all along.

The lessons you learn fulfill one of two goals: God is either grounding you in your basic faith or He's preparing to launch you into something greater. In this regard, adversity comes whether you want it or not and whether you think you need it or not. It's not the result of something you did or a choice you made; it's the result of God's using the experience to develop you in a specific direction. It presents you with two possible choices, each of which sends you in a different direction and reflects your response to God's intent. You can rebel by turning away from God or you can rest in the assurance that God's way will eventually become clear.

Adversity can bring you to pain. It may be sudden and immense — victims of natural disasters understand first hand the overwhelming impact on their lives when everything is taken away all at once. Shock at the loss blocks out reason and you feel like you've gone far past the breaking point.

But you may never experience really terrible things. Much of the adversity you face is probably of a lower intensity, wearing on you over time like water eroding a rock rather than crashing waves. It takes the form of an ongoing stressor that can make you feel like you're dangling from a ledge or trapped in a car perched halfway over a cliff — not overwhelming at the time but something that could give at any moment. You may have experienced that when you were sweating layoffs at work or waiting up for a child who was late getting back from a party.

Stressful conditions can tempt you to despair for your particular situation and cloud the big picture. When we despair for our own situations, it's easy to think we're the only ones experiencing it and come to believe we alone have to resolve it.

We're tempted to ignore God's plans and power, and the hustle of this "do more with less" era makes it a common feeling.

Adversity as I'm using it in this book isn't persecution, spiritual warfare, or even discipline for sin. It's simply the result of living in an imperfect world. When you read about adversity being other than just bad news, you often read about it in the context of people overcoming it and attributing their success in life to the strength of character developed in those earlier struggles. Mike Utley created a foundation to support research on spinal injuries after suffering a crippling injury as a professional football player, and Ray Charles' music immortalized him in spite of his blindness.

It therefore affects your character by reminding you that you're not in control. When I received some training in the martial art of jujitsu, the first thing I learned was how to fall without hurting myself. Central to the fighting art was the assumption that learning to get up after falling was foundational to becoming an effective fighter. Realizing you're not in control motivates you to develop habits and responses that allow you to bounce back when adversity knocks you down.

And your memory of the experience can therefore serve as a reminder that adversity can lead to greater things. An Internet search turned up Enterprise, Alabama, which has a statue of a boll weevil. Many years ago, the pest wiped out that area's cotton production, the staple of that area's economy. The resulting changes the people had to make created a more diverse economy that became even richer than before, so much so the citizens erected the statue to remind themselves of how that adversity actually forced them into something better.

But God wants to use adversity for something even greater. Adversity builds and reveals character because, whatever the situation, it puts you in a position where God is your only recourse. Your character becomes stronger because your growth is related to your readiness to remember there's a higher goal for you. Initially, you might think only of your present discomfort, but later, your ability to look toward a higher goal becomes more ingrained as a habit, resulting in greater endurance.

That something greater is a greater impact on the world, not just your own life. Horatio Spafford was a nineteenth century businessman who endured more than anyone should. Losing his real estate holdings in the Great Chicago Fire and later his four daughters in a shipwreck, we could understand if he gave way to despair. Instead, he wrote the lyrics to one of the greatest hymns of the faith, "It is Well with My Soul," that inspires and consoles even today. Expressing confidence in God in all circumstances, this hymn's title underscores the attitude toward adversity that positions you for greater things.

So adversity is one of God's ways to build your character. It's not a consequence of your choices, I've heard it said, but God's choice to make you consequential. But it works only if you choose to treat it as a stewardship opportunity, an opportunity to receive a blessing and use it to benefit others. This allows you to tap into the power of turning even unfavorable circumstances into blessing.

Adversity is inevitable. You know the refrigerator will break some time and you know the more you drive on the highways, the greater your risk of being in a traffic wreck. Because of that, you know you should prepare for it. Athletes first train with light workloads and then progress to greater challenges, and students start with elementary subjects before progressing to higher levels.

Preparation includes learning from the experiences of others. Vicarious learning helps you develop responses ahead of time. It also helps you reflect on your past responses to adversity. Learning from the experiences of others includes reading and being mentored. It also reassures you that you're not alone in your experiences and that there's a way out.

It also includes practical measures like saving money in an emergency fund, setting aside supplies to get you through a natural disaster, and having a first aid kit in the car. It includes avoidance measures like locking your door at night and turning off the stove when you leave home. It can be as simple for men as moving your wallet from your back pocket to your front pocket to avoid pickpockets.

In this day and age adversity can be digital. Our credit card company called us to check on some recent expense and we discovered someone had used our credit card number to buy some cell phones. You also read about personal data being stolen from businesses and government agencies.

Preparation has another purpose besides protecting you from the consequences of adversity. It allows you to recover more quickly so you can be available to help others. Have you ever been in the middle of repairing something when you realized you needed a specific tool? And what a relief it was when a neighbor happened to have that tool to loan you. That neighbor was prepared for such a situation and was therefore something of a blessing for you.

Humor can help you turn difficult situations into stewardship opportunities. The mother of England's Queen Elizabeth, the beloved Queen Mum, once said of bomb damage to Buckingham Palace during the London Blitz in World War Two, "Now I feel I can look the East End in the face."

And a man who had been one of the US Navy's elite SEALs, the Sea, Air, and Land special operations warriors who endure some of the harshest military training in the world, was told he had a form of cancer that only had a thirty percent recovery rate. "That's okay," he said, "There was only a 10 percent chance of my becoming a SEAL."

In the midst of adversity, you can tell how much you've developed by how you act. In the face of small stressors, do you turn to comfort food? Do you feel frustrated because of your discomfort? First, it's normal to feel stressed and to have those thoughts in the forefront of your mind. And it's not unusual to complain to God or even lose your temper. But how did it compare to your previous experiences? In God's calculations, you may not be perfect, but progress in the right direction counts.

Suffering can be a consequence

Suffering is one of the words you probably use to describe difficult circumstances. Let's give it a specific definition to understand how certain circumstances help you grow in specific ways. As a circumstance in which you can boast, suffering includes the difficult circumstances that are the results of your choices directly related to your unfinished business and your faith. Those results either validate your understanding of your unfinished business because you're having a positive effect on the world or they get you back on track in pursuing your unfinished business because you got off course.

You may suffer because some in this world hate what you and your unfinished business stand for — and if it can happen to Jesus, it can happen to you. By choosing to pursue your unfinished business, you become for some "an aroma from death to death, to the other an aroma from life to life" (II Corinthians 2:16). In other words, pursuing your unfinished business threatens some and reassures others. The suffering you experience comes from those who feel threatened — if you weren't a threat, you wouldn't suffer at their hands. In fact, they might even commend you for holding back.

Because you're a threat to forces that would keep this world from God when you pursue your unfinished business, Satan could be waging spiritual warfare. Consider Daniel's experience. Here was someone whom God was using, yet he had a time when he didn't get a response from God. After Daniel had been praying for three weeks, an angel appeared, explaining "the prince of the kingdom of Persia was withstanding me" (Daniel 10:13). But because Daniel persisted in prayer, he became an instrument for transmitting God's prophecies to His people.

As he did with Daniel, Satan targets your relationship with God to make you ineffective. This is literally your center of gravity, that part of the spiritual battlefield where you want to "overwhelmingly conquer" (Romans 8:37). Don't be surprised, therefore, if you experience similar things when you become more effective in pursuing your unfinished business.

But you could also suffer if you deviate from your unfinished business or from your faith. That's because sin has consequences. Suffering can come upon you to correct your direction as it did throughout the Old Testament history of Israel, at constant war with peoples along her borders and conquered by superpowers that passed through the region because her people kept turning to idol-worship and had not followed through on the full conquest of Canaan that God had ordered.

A person enduring suffering for pursuing his or her unfinished business is like a special operations soldier behind enemy lines. Having demonstrated great skill and conditioning, special operations soldiers go behind enemy lines to disrupt enemy operations and even rescue others from captivity by an enemy. When you read about spectacular operations and rescues in war, you most likely have read about the exploits of special operations soldiers even though the news may not have reported it because of security classifications.

So if you're suffering because of your commitment to your unfinished business, you know you've been given a special mission and must see it through. It's like the spirit behind an order attributed to General George Marshall, the United States' top general in World War Two, who said," I want an officer for a secret and dangerous mission. I want a West Point football player" in a tribute to the character-building qualities commonly ascribed to sports. You've been prepared for a mission and have the wherewithal to see it through.

So suffering validates your choices regarding your unfinished business. While I'm sure you'd rather have your choices validated in other ways, suffering gives you a clear and objective way to know you're headed in the right direction. You should "Consider it all joy" (James 1:2) because you know you made right decisions and developed in the ways God wants for you.

You can therefore expect to face hard times because of your faith. You'll see the wicked prosper, and you'll be challenged and even discriminated against because you didn't hide your beliefs. Asaph assures you, however, that God owns the final outcome, discovering that while the wicked are "always at ease" (Psalm 73:12), he was reassured after entering "the sanctuary of God; Then I perceived their end" (Psalm 73:17).

And suffering also tells you when you've fallen short. I heard a pastor say, "If you're not desperately seeking God, He puts you in desperate circumstances." This is the discipline that brings you back in line because it reminds you that it's not about you. While not comfortable, it's still a good thing God does it.

Imagine if God let us go our own ways instead of bringing us up short and getting us back on track. It would be the spiritual equivalent of being a hiker lost in the woods, wandering off course and getting more disoriented. The Bible explains it best, saying "those whom the Lord loves He disciplines" (Hebrews 12:6), so you can better pursue the unfinished business he set before you.

Suffering comes in many forms when others oppose you. The potential for physical suffering caused by others is always present, especially in other parts of the world where extremist feelings run high. The music group DC Talk published a modern book of martyrs commemorating those who were martyred for their faith. Other forms of suffering revolve around making you feel like a second-class person, mocking you for your susceptibility to ignorant beliefs and infantilizing you with comments and non-verbal cues.

The suffering that comes from spiritual warfare, Satan trying to hinder you, requires much discernment. Too often, people attribute their difficulties to spiritual warfare when in fact those difficulties were self-inflicted. It's important to be open and honest with yourself and God to ensure you get to the root cause in order to make the right response.

And while people who oppose you typically do it because human nature naturally resists God's call, spiritual warfare can be waged through them as well. Whatever form it takes, the goal is to make you feel inadequate for the task and cause you to abandon your unfinished business. And that opposition can be wearying and therefore calls for pacing yourself. The US Army has incorporated rest planning into its combat operations because soldiers need to be refreshed. And you do too.

Elijah, for example, was weary from opposition when he complained to God "I alone am left" (I Kings 19:10). This came after his triumph against 400 priests and prophets of Baal, the god that Israel's queen Jezebel was introducing into the culture. Israel's king, Ahab, married the Phoenician princess Jezebel that no doubt cemented ties with Phoenicia and allowed her to bring her worship of Baal into Israel.

Even after successfully confronting Baal worship by publicly calling down fire from God to consume a sacrifice where hundreds of Jezebel's priests failed, Elijah finally broke after enduring relentless threats from the queen and fled into hiding. He was at a point of desperation, even asking God to take his life. But God not only assured him there were 7,000 devoted followers (I Kings 19:18), God helped him rest and recover.

Sometimes God is disciplining you. When you associate a difficult time with having done something wrong, remember "those whom the Lord loves He disciplines" (Hebrews 12:6). But there's a difference between being prepared for future work and getting back on track. Certainly, God wants you back on track because He has future plans for you, but the difference is the same as between students moving on to advanced studies and students going through remedial subjects. The work is more basic. Paul expressed it as the difference between milk and solid food, saying in Hebrews 5:12, "you have need again for someone to teach you the elementary principles of the oracles of God, and you have come to need milk and not solid food."

But even if suffering comes from wrong choices, it's not cause to judge the sufferer. If judging sufferers for their wrong choices was the norm, great services like the Union Gospel Mission, crisis pregnancy centers, and halfway houses wouldn't exist. So even if suffering came from wrong choices, the response should be for restoration. In all cases, let unconditional love prevail.

Growth can come from suffering because, like adversity, it causes you to acknowledge that you're not in control and throws you onto God. By validating your choices about your unfinished business, your suffering reminds you that "God causes all things to work together for good to those who love God, to those who are called according to His purpose" (Romans 8:28). That reminder strengthens your trust in God because it keeps your present discomfort from distracting you from the higher goal before you. By now, you've noticed that adversity and suffering have much in common in how they cause you to grow. The end result, a stronger focus on God, can become a beacon because those around you witness your stewardship of such circumstances.

But more than adversity, suffering shows others how you, in your faith, are a steward of difficult situations. Because it's the result of your choices about your unfinished business, others know why you're facing difficulty and watch your response to see if it's consistent with what you profess. This kind of scrutiny can even show up in the media as looking for hypocrisy in public figures who speak according to their beliefs.

But you can turn this scrutiny into an opportunity for stewardship of the experience. Remember that stewardship is using what has been entrusted to you to produce a return in line with the owner's wishes. By being a steward of your situation in a way that's consistent with the values shoring your unfinished business, you can influence others to investigate the source of your faith.

You're the evidence at a trial and God is in the dock. So that scrutiny has impact. One of the church fathers, Tertullian, is supposed to have said, "The blood of martyrs is the seed of the church," because the example of the early Christians in the face of persecution convinced others their faith was genuine and that the object of their faith was real.

Suffering can also change you if you made wrong decisions. It could be the predictable consequence of those decisions — deciding to cheat on tax returns, for example, can result in a jail sentence — or it can be a God-ordained consequence like financial loss after an extended period of not financially supporting God's work.

The memory of such a negative experience attached to a specific decision can act as a deterrent to future acts. But the intent is less to deter future acts and more to realign your thinking. When I hike in the wilderness, I found that it doesn't take much effort to get back on course if I make the corrections early enough. But if I don't make those corrections until later, the adjustment must be that much more drastic.

You might be familiar with Charles Sheldon's great book, *In His Steps*, which describes how several characters began to live according to the answers to the question, "What would Jesus do?" even if the results were negative. And many people sport bracelets inspired by that story to remind themselves to ask that question. That's because following Jesus' example is the first task in preparing yourself to be a steward of suffering in ways that are consistent with your professed values.

Part of that example includes choosing to dwell in the way of suffering if it comes to you because of your choices in pursuing your unfinished business. Jesus chose to dwell in the way of suffering after praying that the task of enduring the crucifixion be taken from Him. In Gethsemane, He spent all night asking God to free Him from that fate. Yet he accepted the task. Your acceptance of your suffering can create opportunities to influence others.

This also includes planning your responses ahead of time. You know the community in which you live, so you can probably predict how you would be treated for taking a stand on specific things. That means you can commit to responding in specific ways. If you blow the whistle on unethical practices at work, you might suffer retaliation. If you object to the use of certain books at school, you might be called a Nazi. And if you propose to start your own ministry, you might even be called a fool. Even your family might react against you.

The key commitment to make ahead of time, therefore, is the other aspect of Jesus' example: forgiveness. Just as He forgave even those who crucified Him, you have to commit ahead of time to forgive those who react against you and cause you to suffer.

And if you determine that your suffering is a consequence of your falling short, be glad. At least God is still trying to reach you instead of allowing you to go your own way as He did Pharaoh when Moses sought freedom for the Hebrews. This is your time to make a course correction.

Remember you're not alone. Others have gone your way, and some have experienced worse. And if God was their consolation, strength, and focus through it all, He'll be the same for you. Staying connected to a community of like-minded people will keep you in touch with others who have experienced what you're going through. But don't be a passive member. You won't find out who can help you unless you're already involved and making those connections.

Character breakers are hazards for everyone

Temptation and *sin* form the other end of BOASTS, mirroring the impact of blessing and opportunity by showing you how you can get off course from your unfinished business. Yet because God gives second chances, those times in your life can become blessings for others because your experience can show others they're not alone in what they're going through and can give them a model of how God can turn them around. The good that comes about is your ability to tell others how God rescued you from those situations. However, it's better not to get into those situations in the first place because even though God can pull you out of those dire straits, you can't erase the consequences of going down those paths.

Temptation is a desire to do things your way

You read earlier that opportunity is the set of choices before you to do things God's way. But that's only half the picture. There are options available to you to do things your way. You're tempted when you're presented with choices to establish ownership of your life without reference to God. To be tempted is to be faced with choices to do things your way.

One of the ultimate questions before you is who gets ownership of your life. Everyone has a boss, and Jesus said you can only serve one master. Temptation is the set of choices that seem to make you your own boss, but David reminds you about the direction of your unfinished business, that the one "who walks with integrity, and works righteousness, And speaks truth in his heart" (Psalm 15:2) is the one who resists temptation.

You're tempted when you recognize a desire for something that diverts you from your unfinished business. Unlike our definition of opportunities, temptation highlights choices emphasizing the self and its appetites. A delicious-looking bowl of cookies cuts through your natural need to satisfy your body's hunger as well as knowledge about the benefits of healthy foods to awaken a desire to gorge yourself on those treats. The object of your desire usually isn't wrong in itself, but temptation makes wrongly using it an attractive proposition.

Temptation can also come from the devil who knows your weaknesses and tries to distract you from your unfinished business. It doesn't take much. Temptation offers you the illusion of getting what you want or achieving your objectives without stretching to build your character. You just have to have good intentions.

In numerous encounters, Jesus cut to the chase, telling the man who wanted to bury his father before starting as a disciple to "allow the dead to bury their own dead" (Matthew 8:22) and challenging the rich young ruler who wanted to know how to gain eternal life to "sell all you possess and give to the poor, and you will have treasure in heaven; and come, follow Me" (Mark 10:21). It's not that He wanted the one to treat his family callously and the other to bankrupt himself, it's that He wanted them to choose not to pursue their unfinished business on their own terms. He wanted them to undergo the character development that begins by becoming God's friend.

Dealing with diabetes has given me a deeper perspective on wrestling with temptation. It was easy enough to feel superior to people who wrestled with vices like smoking and alchoholism. I neither smoked nor drank. But diabetes has forced me to admit that I avoided those vices because of my personality. I neither smoked nor drank because I didn't like the taste of cigarettes and alcoholic beverages, not because I had the willpower that comes from the strength of convictions.

Diabetes showed me how powerful temptation can be when my desires focus on an object. Anything with carbohydrates, that is, starches like bread and chips and sugar like candy and cola, are especially destructive to me because of their high carbohydrate content. The insidiousness of the disease is in how it works inside the body without showing outward symptoms.

Diabetes, the type 2 I have, means my body doesn't burn off the glucose from these foods as quickly as it used to, leaving the glucose to circulate in my blood and silently destroy nerves and organs. The damage doesn't show up for years and by then it's too late, ranging from nerve damage to circulatory problems and finally resulting in kidney damage, blindness, and amputation. A doctor once told me he wouldn't wish diabetes on his worst enemy.

For me, that chocolate cheese cake or bagel with cream cheese may taste delicious, but the glucose that comes from those foods will lead to terrible things some time later if I don't manage my diet appropriately. I know this. And yet, even though I know about those consequences, the temptation is still strong. The lure of those desserts and snacks is powerful, drawing me to the pantry time and again, even when I know what I'm doing to my body.

Temptation can play on your legitimate interest in fulfilling your needs but makes the desire grow by persuading you that the object of your desire is the gateway to happiness. Just attain the object of your desire and everything will fall into place. I'm notorious in our family for looking at fancy gadgets as the key to a better life. Want food to taste good? A new set of kitchen gadgets will do the trick for me. Want to play the guitar well? A fancy electric guitar will surely bring out my dormant musical talent. Temptation plays on that tendency by making a need seem greater than it really is and turning that which would fulfill the need into an object of desire.

Temptation also works because satisfaction of needs is temporary. After you've eaten, you're hungry again. You go to bed to rest, get up in the morning, and are tired at the end of the day, repeating the cycle. Temptation can make you think gratifying those needs instead of pursuing your unfinished business will somehow break the cycle and permanently satisfy those needs.

And it becomes more powerful because it presents you with a variety of ways to achieve gratification. It's not a coincidence that Jesus said the way to destruction is broad and the way to life is narrow. Temptation shows you a cornucopia of possibilities, all of which lead away from your unfinished business. Imagine winning a free shopping spree at your favorite large shopping mall, huge bookstore, or large supermarket filled with every sort of food. There are usually a multitude of options that could crowd out the few best choices.

What makes temptation work is also what makes temptation inevitable. Because you have needs you must satisfy, you might be tempted to satisfy them in ways that distract you from your unfinished business. It may sound trite, but temptation is a fact of life. At issue is how you respond. And your response reveals your level of preparation because the inevitability and ubiquity of temptation mean you can prepare for it. You can take specific steps to inoculate yourself in advance, so you can come through the test.

Temptation isn't coercion. It's not a gun to your head forcing you to do something, and it's not something you're predestined to do. You may be tempted to lose your temper, but you can't point to the color of your hair and say it's a family trait to excuse such an outburst. It's a choice presented to you for which you're responsible.

God doesn't send temptation your way either. In fact, James flatly states that God "does not tempt anyone" (James 1:13). It may seem that way, however, because of its inevitability. But that's because you live in a fallen world populated by fallen people, and temptation is simply part of the environment in which you move.

Nor does being faced with temptation mean you've done something wrong. Martin Luther said the difference between temptation and sin is that while you can't stop the birds from flying overhead, you can keep them from nesting in your hair. In other words, facing temptation isn't wrong, but acting on it is. In fact, you can look at it as an indicator to see if your desire to pursue your unfinished business has grown stronger than your desire to fulfill short term gratification.

Even though temptation itself isn't wrong, it can still lead to feelings of guilt. Because we're continually tempted, it's easy to think there's something wrong with us. It's easy to look at others and wonder why they seem to have their lives so together. But only God can see the true state of everyone's lives and it's a certainty that everyone is experiencing issues with temptation. Tolstoy wrote in *Anna Karenina*, "Happy families are all alike; every unhappy family is unhappy in its own way." Well, everyone is tempted in his or her own way, the temptation targeting each one's desires. So you're not alone.

But if your response to temptation keeps you on track with your unfinished business, you then have an opportunity to influence others positively. Let's go back to an earlier event in Joseph's story. The Bible story of Joseph and Potiphar's wife illustrates the consequences of staying on course. Potiphar was a high ranking Egyptian officer who acquired Joseph as a household slave after Joseph was sold into slavery by his brothers.

Joseph soon attracted the attention of that Egyptian military officer's wife. After he resisted her advances, she finally accused Joseph of trying to attack her, an accusation that put him in jail. The subsequent events in that story put him in position as Pharaoh's highest official and set the stage for saving Egypt and his family from famine, a family that eventually became the nation of Israel. Because you set an example by your response, others have something tangible to which they can refer when faced with similar situations.

Even before encountering a situation requiring a response, therefore, you can prepare yourself. Understanding the nature of temptation, you can anticipate the situations where you're most likely to encounter it. By reflecting on your character and understanding your weaknesses and predilections, you can expect that temptation will attack you in those areas.

The first step therefore is preventive — avoid situations where you're likely to be tempted. When I worked in a bank, we were required to take time away for seven consecutive days and not make contact with anyone or do any of our work. That extended absence was designed to make it difficult for bank employees to embezzle money and therefore less likely to be tempted.

One way to make prevention more tolerable is to find wholesome substitutes. I used to drink soft drinks full of sugar but now enjoy diet colas as part of a diet to manage diabetes. Some brands actually taste better to me now than the non-diet varieties, so keeping myself from that kind of temptation is easier to do and helps me control the carbohydrate intake that's bad for a diabetic.

But preventive measures may also call for something as drastic as breaking away from peers until you've developed enough to be around them again. Jesus felt that the potential consequences from giving in to temptation were so dire and preventive measures so effective, He said, "If your right hand makes you stumble, cut it off" (Matthew 5:30). If you can develop a vision of what's truly at stake, the positive impact on the world that comes from pursuing your unfinished business effectively, you can create a greater motivation to make the break.

If you're confronted with temptation, flee. There's a pond in a neighbor's property that's home to a number of ducks. They enjoy walking around the property, but whenever a stranger approaches, they run into the water. The Bible is replete with admonishments to flee temptation. Paul told his readers to "Flee immorality" (I Corinthians 6:18). Don't try to stand and resist because after a while, it won't seem so bad. I find it easy to rationalize indulging in rich foods by saying I can get back on my diet tomorrow.

Sin is doing things your way

The flip side of blessings, sin is how we characterize our stewardship of what God has given us when we choose to do things our way. We're human and sin is the strongest word out there to say we do wrong things and to communicate the seriousness of straightening out those situations into which we get ourselves. Let's face it: there are wrong things by any moral code as well as by your own moral code and they'll derail your unfinished business.

When we sin, we've acted on the temptation to gratify our desires in a self-focused way. It's the outcome of establishing ownership of our lives without reference to God. The opposite of blessings, there are times when we've fallen down by making choices that fall short of the mark. David's confession guides us out of that morass, acknowledging and pleading, "Against You, You only, I have sinned And done what is evil in Your sight... Create in me a clean heart, O God, And renew a steadfast spirit within me" (Psalm 51:4, 10).

So the act of sin isn't the end of the story. It includes consequences we have to deal with. Like an iceberg, the act is only the tip seen above the water, the gratification from accommodating a particular desire, but the consequences are the rest of the iceberg, the massive structure under the water that sinks ships. It's the downhill process James outlined for his readers, "Then when lust has conceived, it gives birth to sin; and when sin is accomplished, it brings forth death" (James 1:15).

When strolling through a shopping mall parking lot with my daughter, we saw that the root of one of the trees had broken through the asphalt, forcing its way through the ground and causing the asphalt to bulge up until it broke. I mentioned to her that sin was like that root — we can keep it out of sight for a while, but the consequences eventually break through the surface of your life. Of course, like all children, she was ready with a comment on my brilliant sermonette. "Yeah, Dad," she rolled her eyes and said, "just like your need to turn everything into a lecture."

Sin can be spectacularly disastrous like David's adultery with Bathsheba, his initial sin causing a pregnancy that could jeopardize orderly succession to the throne and compounding itself into a massive cover-up topped off with murder. Although he had sent his army to war, David stayed back in Jerusalem instead of leading his troops at the front. Lounging in the evening, he saw Bathsheba, brought her to his palace, and seduced her. And shortly afterwards, Bathsheba, whose husband Uriah was still at the front, announced she was pregnant.

The writer of II Samuel then tells us David brought Uriah back on the pretext of reporting about the campaign, hoping the soldier would spend time with his wife and provide a plausible cause for Bathsheba's pregnancy. Who was this Uriah? One of David's thirty mighty men, Uriah had gained a reputation as a fierce warrior and strong leader. Being named among the thirty mighty men meant he had distinguished himself in battle with feats of courage, a corps of exemplars equivalent to the United States military's Medal of Honor recipients.

And this Uriah lived up to his reputation as an honorable man when he came back to Jerusalem, staying away from his wife because the other soldiers couldn't be with their families as well. So David arranged for Uriah to be killed in battle. And after Uriah's death and Bathsheba's period of mourning, David completed the cover-up by bringing her to the palace as one of his wives.

Sin, therefore, can lead to more sin, David ultimately betraying one of his most loyal and valuable subjects to cover up his act. Although the Bible is silent, I have to think that tongues wagged after Bathsheba arrived in the palace. I don't think David was as successful in covering up his sin as he hoped because those kinds of secrets are impossible to keep for long. We can get into similar trouble — the sin we think we successfully hid really isn't hidden.

That means we have to acknowledge our own vulnerability. If anyone would have had the character to keep from such actions, it was David. Anointed to replace Saul as king when he was still a teenager, it was clear God considered David His friend. David's subsequent actions like confronting Goliath without armor and killing the giant with a sling and pebble showed he fully understood his relationship with God and was willing to follow through.

David had also demonstrated he could see from God's perspective. Recall that he spent his young manhood running away from Saul because that old king was jealous of David's popularity to the point of murder. And while he was running from Saul, he twice refrained from killing the king when presented the opportunity, a forbearance that reflected his willingness to wait on God's timetable rather than trying to seize the kingship.

All that made David God's blessing to others as well. Besides winning great victories for Israel and uniting the nation when he became king, David created a literary legacy in his Psalms that still comfort and inspire people centuries later. His psalms range from thanksgiving to pleas for protection. He asks God for vindication, complains about injustice, and offers lyrical praises. Their words help us navigate the path of our unfinished business.

So by the time David saw Bathsheba, he had already shown he was fully engaged in pursuing his unfinished business. Yet he sinned. And his fall teaches us why our unfinished business remains unfinished: although God regards us already as whom He wants us to be, He wants us to understand there's a path yet to travel with distractions that can draw us from it.

But in most cases, sin works in a subtly progressive manner until it breaks out into full view, much like that root growing through the asphalt in the parking lot or the excess glucose from my diabetes damaging nerves and organs. The damage is being done out of sight until one day it reaches a tipping point and erupts. That's one reason why the wicked seem to prosper — in the limited time you have on earth and with the finite perspective you have as a human, you can't see what's really happening in their lives except for the occasional sensational media coverage of some scandal.

Sin is common to all, but that doesn't excuse it from being so common. It can take any number of forms, from forgetting to do what you should to outright rebellion. One form is simply missing a mark you were aiming for, failing to live up to a standard. I learned how this works when I took up skeet shooting. Hitting the clay pigeon requires attention to stance, a good lead, and positioning the shotgun so it's already in place to fire. Disregarding any of those fundamentals yields a missed target. Meeting a certain standard, then, doesn't happen on its own. It calls for a deliberate decision to hit the mark.

Sin might take the form of an offense that ruptures a relationship. Adultery is a vivid example, but more common instances include the hurt caused by gossip or not being a true friend. It can be an oversight in another area that hurts others. After a putting on a successful conference, I neglected to thank some people who worked particularly hard. I apologized later, but my failure to pay attention to those details in the beginning was still hurtful.

We can also sin by being so proud that we set ourselves above the law. That is, we can think some standards don't apply to us. In some cases, it can involve rationalizing that the ends justify the means and in other cases, it can show up as refusal to abide by common moral principles. According to Frederick Douglass, for example, a great evil of slavery was that it gave absolute power to slave owners, corrupting them until they saw nothing wrong with actions like whipping slaves after church services.

But ultimately, we don't want to know the depths to which people can sink when they become mired in sin. A number of police officers I know seem to have a more jaundiced view of the world than me. I think that's because of what they have to see. Just when they think they've seen it all, something worse comes along. That by itself should be sufficient reason to run the other way when you're tempted.

But as bad as sin is, it's not a boundary marker that gives us license to judge others. While we need the wisdom to discern right from wrong, the presence to walk away from wrong, and the courage to warn others when they're straying, we don't have the leeway to use that knowledge to set ourselves above others. We warn others because we want them to avoid disaster, not because we want to feel superior. So bringing sin to someone's attention is a diagnosis and prescription, not a condemnation.

Sin is corrosive. That is, over time, sin can corrode our perception. When materials corrode, they deteriorate because their components have gone through a chemical reaction with the environment. You're most familiar with rust when iron combines with air to create a reddish-brown powder on the surface. Corrosion weakens the material and makes it more likely to break under stress. Sin can corrode moral foundations until they become brittle enough to break.

Sin is also erosive. The strongest rocks, for example, can wear away from the incessant action of water. What was once a flat area in northern Arizona is now the Grand Canyon. Sin is erosive because it keeps eating away, breaking us down by making it easier to become involved in greater sin. One instance may be small and seem inconsequential, but it becomes easier to commit the next sin. And then it's easier to commit sins with more obvious impact. By the time we realize how far we've gotten, we've formed new habits and ingrained new practices.

When you identify sin in your life, you should acknowledge the actions causing you to miss the mark and change direction. My skeet instructor explained how to identify which fundamentals of stance and gun position I violated to make my shooting more accurate. Repentance is the spiritual equivalent, a process of understanding where you fell short, acknowledging those instances, and then changing course. It's an acknowledgement of what you've been doing and a turning away from it.

King David repented after understanding what he had done to Uriah. Confronted by Nathan the prophet, it became clear to David how far he had drifted. The famous Psalm 51, a vivid acknowledgment of his culpability, drew God's forgiveness because David fully admitted guilt. This psalm has become an example of the self examination involved in repentance.

You may have identified sin because you experienced suffering as one of the consequences. If so, consider yourself blessed and go the way of repentance. That's one of God's ways of reminding you of your unfinished business and getting you back on track. He eventually leaves those alone who want to be left alone in their sin. The chronicler, some think it was Ezra, wrote about Zedekiah, a king of Judah just before a massive Chaldean attack, who "stiffened his neck and hardened his heart against turning to the Lord God of Israel" (II Chronicles 36:13). At that point, God lets them have their way.

But if you repent, you can turn the experience into a lesson for others, becoming an example so others can see they're not alone in their situations. That's why the accounts of people who came out of bad backgrounds are so compelling. We see ourselves in those accounts, either actually being in those situations or realizing the difference is only a matter of degree. It underscores God as a giver of second chances because repentance can let others see God at work.

4

SEE FROM *GOD'S PERSPECTIVE* BY MAKING HIS PRIORITIES YOUR PRIORITIES

Being out of the wilderness doesn't mean you're in the Promised Land, so although God uses your circumstances to make you the friend He wants you to be, one who can find Him in those circumstances, He also uses them to change your perspective. That changed perspective is knowing what to do about your friendship with God — your faith turned into knowledge. In other words, it's making His priorities your priorities, the natural next step after God turns you into the friend He wants you to be so you can stay the course.

Setting your priorities and keeping them in order helps you stay on course because well ordered priorities demonstrate that you can see from God's perspective and avoid choices that gratify self-interest. Just as heroes are prepared before setting off on their quests, God has begun your preparation by giving you an example to follow — Jesus Christ. By following Jesus' example, your preparation will ground you in the qualities you need to pursue your unfinished business and perfect you in exercising those qualities so you can keep your life balanced and on track.

The Bible fast forwards through Jesus' adolescence, saying only that during the time between His twelfth birthday and His emergence onto the public stage He "kept increasing in wisdom and stature, and in favor with God and men" (Luke 2:52). That single glimpse of Jesus' growth summarizes a time when He was maturing and getting ready to embark on His mission, hinting at how God can ground and perfect you in those dimensions so you can stay on track with your unfinished business. Keep in mind, of course, that although Jesus, being perfect already, subjected Himself to the process of human growth to show us how to live, our own growth will be a life-long process.

According to that verse, Jesus matured in four dimensions: wisdom (intellectual), stature (physical), favor with God (spiritual), and favor with man (social). And after God has called you to your unfinished business by making you His friend, He helps you turn that relationship of faith into knowledge in those same dimensions in your life, helping you learn what to do about your faith in the real world. But missing from that list are areas like career, finances, and family.

That's because the four major dimensions encompass those areas. Think about how you employ the social dimension in your career, contributing to the work of teams, guiding your subordinates, and relating to your bosses. Think about how the intellectual dimension affects your personal financial decisions like developing budgets, managing your spending, and making investment decisions. The spiritual dimension influences how you raise a family in the values you teach and the example you set. And of course, it would be hard to be effective in any of those areas without physical well-being.

5

JESUS' LIFE IS THE BASIS
FOR MAKING GOD'S PRIORITIES YOUR PRIORITIES

Because pursuing your unfinished business sets you on a particular course, you have some tough choices to make. It might be straightforward to recognize wrong things that might derail you (avoiding them is another question), but it's much more challenging when faced with choices, all of which might be beneficial. Several years ago, for example, there was concern about youth sports activities taking place on Sundays, forcing families to decide between going to church and letting their children take part in something worthwhile. Many choices will be like that.

Is there a way to go about it that gives you results consistent with the unfinished business God has presented you? There is. You can bring such balance and consistency to your life by developing in those four dimensions because Jesus' example teaches you how to set priorities.

That brief account of Jesus' adolescence is a clue to understanding how to set priorities, its brevity signaling its importance to the gospel writer's general purpose. Luke sandwiched that account between Jesus' pre-teen visit to Jerusalem and Jesus' emergence as a public figure as a 30-year-old. Because Luke compressed that time span of eighteen years into one verse, his writing style suggests how you can prioritize your life.

Most of Luke's gospel is about Jesus' three years of public ministry culminating in his crucifixion. It's clear from the amount of coverage that Luke wanted to focus on Jesus' mission, so it makes sense he devoted most of the gospel to that part of Jesus' life. In other words, Luke prioritized his writing based on

Jesus' mission. You too can prioritize your decisions based on that same mission. So what's this kind of prioritization all about?

I was told that eagles learn to fly by being pushed out of the nest. After a period of care and feeding by its mother when the eaglet has grown to point where its wings are strong enough to support it in flight, its mother pushes it out of the nest. Falling to earth, the eaglet flaps its wings and succeeds in flying.

I've also read that predators like lions raised in captivity have to be trained how to hunt before they can be released into the wild. Because they weren't raised in the wild, they never learned how to hunt and would starve if their human keepers didn't somehow teach those skills. Everything has a purpose, and growth must be linked to the purpose. That's the secret of prioritization — know the purpose and priorities fall into place.

Jesus Himself showed the relationship of purpose and priorities during a childhood visit to Jerusalem in which He was separated from His parents and missed their departure home. Responding to His parents who found Him in the temple after a frantic search, Jesus pointed out, "Did you not know that I had to be in My Father's house?" (Luke 2:49). Other translations use the phrase, "my Father's business," both translations showing Jesus' recognition of His mission. Jesus' statement and His subsequent public ministry described later in the gospel suggest that He developed in the four dimensions of life in ways that supported His future work. You can prioritize the same way as you grow in the four dimensions of your life.

The scant coverage Luke gave Jesus' growth therefore emphasizes launching, not staying. The gospel writer fast forwarded through those eighteen years because while they *supported* Jesus' mission, they *weren't* Jesus' mission, something Luke wanted to make sure came through in the gospel. Pursuing your unfinished business, therefore, means knowing your mission and prioritizing what you do to support it. This means you can develop in relevant ways if you relate your growth to your unfinished business, reviewing where you are in your growth and then identifying what you have to do to go further.

So pursuing your unfinished business, whatever it is, revolves around what you think about Jesus and how you act on that belief. Jesus put the question to His disciples, "Who do people say that I am?" (Mark 8:27). By this time, Jesus had drawn attention because of His teaching and miracles like feeding thousands of people from food enough only for a single person and healing people from various afflictions. As a result, he was being hailed as the return of one of the great prophets like Elijah.

Thinking about Jesus that way or calling Him a great teacher affects how you view your unfinished business because it describes a belief at odds with what the Bible describes. If you think of Jesus that way, it becomes easy to recast His teachings as guidelines from which you can pick, choosing those you think most applicable.

Think about terrific teachers you had in school and public figures who've written books about self-improvement and personal effectiveness. Did you follow *all* their ideas much less agree with them? More likely, you picked out what seemed relevant to your situation, building a mosaic of ideas gleaned from different thinkers. But C.S. Lewis got to the heart of the matter, saying

> Either this man was, and is, the Son of God: or else a madman or something worse. You can shut Him up for a fool, you can spit at Him and kill Him as a demon or you can fall at His feet and call Him Lord and God. But let us not come with any patronizing nonsense about His being a great human teacher. He has not left that open to us. He did not intend to.

So basing your unfinished business on what you believe about Jesus Christ drives how you act on that belief and governs your choices about your priorities.

Nor is your growth in the four dimensions of your life an end state. While it's true that personal growth is a life-long process, it supports something greater. It's like achieving black belt status in the martial arts. A martial arts instructor explained to me that achieving black belt rank isn't a final goal, it's just a sign the martial artist is finally ready for serious study. In the same way, graduating with a doctorate isn't an end; it's the beginning of serious scholarship. The doctoral program was just the training ground.

John, another gospel writer, told his readers about Jesus' understanding of God, saying, "He has explained Him" (John 1:18). John and Luke understood that Jesus' mission was to draw people to God and wrote their gospels accordingly. Pursuing your unfinished business will have the same effect if you believe that Jesus is more than a great teacher, and you'll bring balance to your life because that belief will help you set your priorities accordingly.

After hearing His disciples describe who people thought Jesus was, He challenged them, asking, "But who do you say that I am?" (Mark 8:29). That's the question you must answer for yourself. Many ideas compete with the Biblical record, challenging the words the gospel writers recorded, so you have to cut through the noise to get to the quiet center that forms your core belief.

Taking Jesus Christ at His word will help organize your life and personal growth, not only bringing a sense of balance but also a conviction that everything you're doing helps you pursue your unfinished business. It will equip you for pursuing your unfinished business because understanding who Jesus Christ is sets you on the path of imitating Him.

Making God's priorities, then, involves taking on God's character in the four dimensions of your life, fulfilling Jesus' command "to be perfect, as your heavenly Father is perfect" (Matthew 5:48). This requirement isn't as shocking as it sounds at first. It isn't shocking because we'd expect God to be perfect

— it would be distressing, for example, to follow the gods of Greek mythology that exhibited all the human frailties like pride and jealousy and had the supernatural power to act on those characteristics.

Nor should it be shocking to have perfection expected in ourselves. For one thing, it's the entry point to becoming God's friend, something He has already provided for through Jesus Christ's crucifixion and resurrection. For another thing, perfection is a state of completion, all aspects of life fully integrated and balanced, toward which you're working. And pursuing your unfinished business, that desire to do something about your friendship with God, moves you forward on that path.

Increase like Jesus to grow

In the short description of Jesus' growth you read earlier, the word "increasing" describes the quality of Jesus' development. It's also how you develop as you make God's priorities your priorities. "Increasing," therefore, is the process by which you learn what it means to apply your faith to your life. More than just the natural accumulation of knowledge you acquire as you get older, "increasing" helps you understand how to integrate your faith into those four dimensions of life.

Something else increases as well: the growth of Jesus Christ's impact on your life. You can improve in the four dimensions of life — intellectual, physical, spiritual, and social — but you can't increase without subordinating them to Jesus. That subordination ensures a consistent direction for your growth because simply improving yourself in those areas leaves you open to falling back into your comfort zone when you were the one making the decisions about who you would be, what you would know, and where you would go.

That's because increasing in those four areas comes from your deepening understanding of who Jesus Christ is. John, the gospel writer, said Jesus explained God, and Jesus Himself challenged his listeners to declare who He is. The word "increase" translates from the original Greek, *prokopto*, in a couple of interesting ways. From its meaning of advancing or going forward, it's used to indicate progress. Paul said of his life before his conversion to Christianity, "I was advancing in Judaism beyond many of my contemporaries among my countrymen, being more extremely zealous for my ancestral traditions" (Galatians 1:14). In that verse, "advancing" is the same word as "increasing" in the Gospel verse describing Jesus' adolescence.

That means you can make progress in the wrong direction as well. When Paul cautions his readers to "avoid worldly and empty chatter, for it will lead to further ungodliness" (II Timothy 2:16), the phrase "lead to" is the same as "increasing" but shows how easily you can increase in the wrong ways. It's similar to the erosive and corrosive effects of sin.

The word also conveys the idea of lengthening out by hammering, and the image is of a smith working with metal. I saw a film once of a sword maker starting with a clump of metal and, by repeatedly heating it and hammering it, turned it into a long gleaming sword blade. So growth is more than just learning more things, it also means experiencing things that shape your character like the circumstances God allows into your life to keep you on the path of your unfinished business. In other words, it's not enough to get some knowledge into your head — you have to make it useful by learning how to apply it in real situations.

Schools know that. After you learn some formulas in chemistry class, for example, your teacher has you perform an experiment in a lab so you can see how those formulas work in actual use. In my chemistry classes in school, for example, we calculated what should happen when we combined certain chemicals and then actually combined those chemicals in the lab to see if we would get what our calculations predicted. That's how God uses circumstances. They're opportunities to internalize what you learned so your actual responses to various situations are actually what God says they ought to be.

One of my favorite Bible chapters, Psalm 1, illustrates the idea of increasing. David says a righteous person "will be like a tree firmly planted by streams of water, Which yields its fruit in its season And its leaf does not wither; And in whatever he does, he prospers" (Psalm 1:3). Like the tree's being well rooted and nourished by water, your growth depends on outside sources as well. As you learned in pursuing your unfinished business, your own growth comes from being grounded in God.

We have a tree on our property that died recently. The ground was too compacted from the heavy equipment that prepared the land for a new house. Not only did the compacted ground not allow enough oxygen to get to the tree's roots, it didn't absorb as much water, letting too much of it run off on the surface. As a result, the tree didn't get the nourishment it needed and died. Your growth too is affected by what you're rooted in.

If you're well rooted, the result of your growth will be fruitful like a tree is fruitful. But trees only produce fruit according to their natures. Apple trees produce apples, and orange trees produce oranges. If you think about it, those trees' purposes aren't to produce certain fruits, it's to be apple, and orange trees. And part of their natures is to produce the right fruit. In other words, the fruit is a byproduct of their simply being what God created them to be.

That means when you pursue the unfinished business God has presented you, the fruit you produce is a byproduct, not the goal, of that endeavor. You're just being the person God expects you to be. For example, parents should raise their children "in the discipline and instruction of the Lord" (Ephesians 6:4), a task that's part of being parents. Children who grow up to be God-fearing and reverent are the fruit of that labor, the byproduct of parents being parents.

And it will be "in its season," that is, according to God's timetable. You can't hurry a tree, and you can't hurry God. You wouldn't want to hurry a medical school in graduating doctors. Instead, you'd want their training to proceed according to the timetable set by the school because you know that's what it takes to produce a fully qualified doctor.

Likewise, pursuing your unfinished business moves according to the timetable God set for it. Your unfinished business may involve having to get an advanced education, something that will take a number of years. Or it may require time in different jobs if you're learning a trade. It may even be a lifelong pursuit like building an organization.

The tree's leaf doesn't wither because it's cared for, and God will care for you as well and lead you to prosperity. That means indestructibility and prosperity are intriguing thoughts about your growth. God has you under His care, and until it's time for you to go home to Him, you'll stay on in this world no matter what happens. But it will be according to His definition of prosperity, not yours or anyone else's, and, as you've already learned, God's definitions of success and achievement are very different from how others see them.

So how does "increasing" work? It's an ongoing growth in understanding how to demonstrate your faith in your life. That's because knowledge remains abstract until you understand how it applies to the reality of your life. I recall sitting through a presentation on employment benefits at work. The presenter listed the main points of health and dental benefits, pointing out amounts of co-payments, scopes of coverage, and procedures for obtaining approval of providers. She also explained the paid vacation benefit, employee discounts, and the retirement program.

When she asked for questions, the new employees peppered her with questions drawn from their own specific situations. The presenter explained to the questioners the parts of the benefits program relevant to their specific situations, the impact of those relevant parts on their specific situations, and how the new employees could take advantage of those benefits in their specific situations. In other words, she understood how the principles governing the benefits program could apply to specific situations and passed that knowledge to the new employees.

Look at how Jesus drilled down from general to specific. One day, an expert in Jewish law tested Jesus, asking Jesus what must be done to inherit eternal life. Talk about broad principles — that question was as broad as broad could get. Jesus narrowed the topic a bit, asking the expert to point out the principles relevant to the question and eliciting two points of connection: to love God and to love one's neighbor as oneself.

But the expert wanted specifics, demanding of Jesus how to tell who qualified as neighbor. After all, as a Jew, the expert knew which God to worship but probably hoped to catch Jesus on a theological fine point. For when Israel conquered Canaan centuries before, God told the Israelites not to mix with people from the other cultures so their religion wouldn't be diluted and their relationship with God weakened. But Israel did, swinging back and forth between God and the pagan deities like a pendulum.

So by the time the expert in Jewish law was born, Israel had been paying the penalty for violating that specific command for a number of centuries, battling the non-Jewish peoples within Israel's borders and being attacked by the various superpowers that built empires. In fact, when the expert was quizzing Jesus, the region had been garrisoned by the forces of the latest superpower, the Roman Empire, for a long time. So you can understand why defining who should be considered a neighbor was a sensitive question. Absorbing the practices of different cultures and creating international alliances had been a costly mistake for the Jews.

So Jesus narrowed the focus even more, telling the famous parable of the Good Samaritan. In that parable, two exemplars of Jewish law, a priest and a Levite, didn't help a man who had been beaten by robbers, but a Samaritan not only helped the man, he also went the extra mile by paying an innkeeper to shelter the victim during the healing period.

Because people of Samaria were just the kind of people Jews felt they shouldn't associate with (people of Samaria were the product of the intermarriage of Israelites and indigenous people and also practiced the Jewish religion differently), Jesus forced the expert to zoom to the most relevant part of the principle — we're all each others' neighbors — and acknowledge how the broad principle applied to a specific part of that expert's life.

Therefore, "increasing" doesn't only help you learn new things, it helps you integrate that knowledge into the four dimensions of life. And as your understanding deepens and your ability to make effective decisions increases, it may seem intuitive. Sometimes you might not be able to explain the rationale of your actions right away any more than champion athletes can explain the details of record-setting performances or great artists can explain the dynamics of their creativity. It just happens because of the "increasing" that took place.

Ask Michelangelo how he created his great sculptures and he would reply, "I saw the angel in the marble and I just chiseled until I set him free." It's not a very illuminating explanation, but it conveys the idea of how his years of study of form and structure became habit. Ask soldiers on the battlefield how they were able to perform magnificent feats of courage, and the best they'll probably be able to tell you is, "My buddies needed help and the training kicked in." They saw a need and their training came out as instinctive action.

So "increasing" isn't a guarantee of material well-being in this world nor is consistent positive progress a certainty. Remember the four dimensions — intellectual, physical, spiritual, and social — are components of who you are, not the spheres in which you operate. So the purpose of increasing in those dimensions is to make you a person with godly habits prepared to turn that knowledge into practice, not a person who strides through this world from triumph to triumph.

In a ringing tribute to people of true faith who went before, the writer of the letter to the Hebrews listed not only triumphs like Israel's conquest of Jericho and David's victories but also noted that

> others experienced mockings and scourgings, yes, also chains and imprisonment. They were stoned, they were sawn in two, they were tempted, they were put to death with the sword; they went about in sheepskins, in goatskins, being destitute, afflicted, ill-treated (men of whom the world was not worthy), wandering in deserts and mountains and caves and holes in the ground. (Hebrews 11:36-38)

Persecution is a grim thing to contemplate, but even today, there are countless people who, while developing godly habits, experience things too terrible to contemplate from the perspective of life in the United States.

There will even be times when you'll fail and have to start again. That's because you're not perfect. Although Jesus overcame temptations during His time on earth, it wasn't to prove that we too can achieve perfection in this life but to demonstrate His perfection and worthiness to be called the Son of God. So this means we're not to judge others' progress. Remember that everyone has feet of clay — just don't let those feet get so big you always trip over them or trip other people.

And what is the outcome of "increasing"? You'll become an effective steward of your circumstances. Paul noted to Christians in Galatia that "the fruit of the Spirit is love, joy, peace, patience, kindness, goodness, faithfulness, gentleness, self-control" (Galatians 5:22). These qualities demonstrate an understanding of how your faith becomes integrated into all aspects of your life.

Let's look at self-control. This habit comes from the broad concept that while "All things are lawful, but not all things are profitable. All things are lawful, but not all things edify" (I Corinthians 10:23) and the knowledge of the consequences of various choices. For example, what you eat and drink affects your body in healthy and unhealthy ways, from cholesterol levels to blood pressure to allergic reactions to intoxication.

Although you may have knowledge about the effects of different foods, it won't do you any good if you haven't refined that knowledge into a habit that helps you withstand the temptation to overindulge in certain foods or drink. It will also steer you to the foods and drink you need for good health. And the stronger your self-control habit is, the more likely it will be that you'll eat the foods and drink the beverages that are best for your body.

So what should you do about it? Knowing that trees yield fruit according to their natures, remember that taking up your unfinished business has made you the kind of person designed to yield the fruit of the Spirit. To keep moving forward, commit to cultivating those fruits; that is, resolve to allow God to use the circumstances that come into your life to help you turn godly knowledge into godly habits.

This allows you to "present yourself approved to God as a workman who does not need to be ashamed, accurately handling the word of truth" (II Timothy 2:15). Just as a workman turns concepts into practical knowledge through study and turns practical knowledge into habit through application, you can achieve the same integration when you increase.

For example, intellectual disciplines like reading will improve your ability to think critically and imaginatively. They'll even improve your ability to communicate because you'll see how other people communicate.

Reading sound books not only gives you knowledge, they also let you experience life vicariously, learning from decisions other people made and finding the relevant points where broad principles connect to specific life situations.

Physical disciplines are easier said than done, involving practices like diet and exercise. And you've heard of spiritual disciplines like prayer and worship that strengthen your faith as well as social disciplines like etiquette that help you demonstrate your consideration for others' feelings.

But you can't do it alone. In acquiring the knowledge you need to integrate faith into all four dimensions, there are things you know and things you don't know. If you know you don't have knowledge in certain areas, you can take steps to get it like reading books, seeking advice, or taking classes. But there is also knowledge you need but don't know you need it. And you'll never know until someone points it out to you. That's what teachers and mentors do.

To increase in the four life dimensions, you must find teachers and mentors who can guide you along the way. Teachers help you acquire knowledge and mentors help you integrate it into your life so you can turn it into habit. They can even be the same person.

In the movies, Luke Skywalker had Obee Wan Kenobee and in real life, Dwight Eisenhower had Brigadier General Fox Connor, with whom the young Eisenhower served. Connor spent time coaching Eisenhower in things military and even showed the young officer how to establish a personal study program for continuing professional development. Eisenhower went on to lead the invasion of France on D-Day in World War Two and was elected President in 1952.

Increase in wisdom for discerning decisions

Increasing in wisdom involves integrating your faith and mind. Sometimes called good judgment, savvy, or common sense, wisdom is more than being smart. It's a way of thinking that goes beyond intellectual achievement. Although your intellect is heavily involved, wisdom is the evidence your intellect is helping you make effective decisions.

65

Wisdom is grounded in what scholars call objective truth, that is, things that are true all the time and everywhere for everyone. I used to tell my children, "There's a time and place for everything, and the time and place for some things is always and everywhere and for other things never and nowhere." The time for objective truth is always, and the place is everywhere.

That's because the other name for objective truth is God, and the image of that truth is Jesus Christ. Remember that our example for increasing in the four life dimensions is not only the one who *explained* God, He is also the one who claimed to *be* God. If you accept His claim, you accept what He says as the standard by which you make decisions.

Once in a while, I have to chastise myself when I realize I forgot to set my socks out the afternoon before after changing out of my work clothes. Because I get up just before sunrise, that means I have to rely on the indoor lights to illuminate the dresser drawers from which I pick my socks for that day. Once in a while, I select what look like navy blue socks to go with my gray trousers but discover later in the day that I actually picked out dark brown socks. Without the sunlight from the afternoon before shining through the bedroom window, navy blue and dark brown can look the same to me.

There's something about sunlight that makes the colors more apparent to human eyes (especially older human eyes like mine) that indoor lighting fails to duplicate. Wisdom is like that sunlight, brightly illuminating the truth of situations because, like sunlight touching all colors of the spectrum, wisdom allows you to range across all aspects of life situations you encounter so you can make the right choices.

Wisdom has a couple of components: critical thinking and assumptions. Critical thinking is what most people associate with wisdom. You learned it in school, mostly by studying logical fallacies. You've applied critical thinking to many situations, and you've been on the receiving end of critical thinking as well. Your mother is probably the greatest critical thinker you'll ever encounter. Remember how she effortlessly demolished your arguments?

"But everyone else is doing it!"

"So if everyone else jumped off a cliff, you would too?"

Critical thinking is a quality God honors and in fact desires. Pointing out that "It is the glory of God to conceal a matter, But the glory of kings is to search out a matter" (Proverbs 25:2), Solomon highlights the gift of reason God has given and the task to which God assigns it. It's a tool God has provided for meeting this world's challenges and for cutting through to the heart of things.

The foundational component of wisdom, however, is the set of assumptions you adopt because that's where your understanding of objective truth resides. Assumptions are beliefs you treat as facts, components of how you look at the world. You can't prove them, but in order to make sense of life, you allow those assumptions to take the place of facts because you simply don't have perfect knowledge.

For example, you may not be able to prove God exists, but if you take it on faith, you treat that belief in God's existence as a fact, and it has huge effects on your life. It moves you to govern your life according to commandments set forth in the book about God (the Bible) and to make decisions based on what you think God would have you do.

You rely on assumptions in everyday situations as well. When you take on debt to buy a house or a car, you assume you'll have a continuous stream of income with which to make the payments. It may seem like a given thing, and you probably take it so much for granted that it seems like a fact, but it's not guaranteed you'll keep your current job or even get a raise in salary. Those are assumptions about the future you make. You may have strong reasons to believe you'll continue to earn money at least at the same level, but you can't say it's a fact.

Assumptions are foundational precisely because you have to choose to believe them. Facts hit you in the face —

whether you like them or not, you have no choice but to acknowledge them as facts. It may seem like it's the difference between, say, counting fence posts on your property and choosing your favorite food. No matter who counts the number of fence posts, there will only be one correct number. But any number of people will have as many different favorite foods. Someone will prefer hamburgers to which someone else will turn up his or her nose and choose smoked salmon.

But deciding which assumptions to accept is much more than personal taste, it's a matter of impact — your choice will dictate the outcome of your decisions. Only the degree of impact is different. Some assumptions are benign, like accepting the weather reporter's prediction for the day and choosing your clothes accordingly, but others are profound, like deciding whether to believe in God.

Therefore, assumptions can have massive consequences. Hitler convinced a nation to accept his assumptions about the superiority of one race over others and led that nation into a world war. But because they're under the surface, assumptions are easy to miss. Your critical thinking skills, a component of wisdom you read about a few paragraphs earlier, can help you find those assumptions.

How else can you think about wisdom? Jesus made an intriguing statement that describes wise people, charging His disciples to "be shrewd as serpents and innocent as doves" (Matthew 10:16) because He was sending them to minister to a world that would take advantage of them. "Shrewd" is also translated as "wise" in other verses.

By charging them to be innocent, He disarmed those disciples because the Sermon on the Mount, which came earlier in the gospel account, prescribed a number of qualities like meekness and forgiveness that encouraged them not to strike back, a very familiar action in human relationships. So the disciples had to be shrewd so they could respond in ways consistent with Jesus' commands.

68

Prudence is another name for that kind of wisdom. The book of Proverbs uses the word to describe people who neither act out nor show off but rather seek knowledge, look before leaping, and avoid evil. There is a practicality to wisdom that can be seen in the rational way wise people live. They don't overspend their earnings, they deliberate before making decisions, and they refer back to the values by which they want to live.

You can think of it as being "street smart" and be struck by that quality being ascribed not just to people who are deliberate, discreet, and disciplined but also to the serpent that persuaded Eve to eat the fruit. Because the serpent is described with the same word in Genesis, you can understand why wisdom has to be anchored to objective truth — the intellectual sharpness of prudence is a tool that cuts both ways.

But the shrewdness that is wisdom reaches it highest form as discernment. You may have heard the illustration of how bank tellers are taught to spot counterfeits by spending their time looking at and handling real money. With discernment, you can "test the spirits to see whether they are from God" (I John 4:1) and tell the counterfeit from the real. At this level of wisdom, you have brought imagination and intellect together using your assumptions as a yoke. In other words, the God of your faith harnesses your intellect and imagination to a higher purpose.

You may have received emails from someone in another country telling a sad story of how the sender's family stood to lose millions of dollars unless the family could get the money into a bank outside the country. And would you, the recipient, be kind enough to help, for which you would be paid a portion of that fortune? This and many other scams have taken people for much money, even their life savings. Discerning people have learned to use their intellects and imaginations to see through these come-ons and protect themselves.

That's why you sometimes hear someone declare, "It doesn't make sense!" when he or she listens to an explanation of

Christian beliefs. It's not supposed to make sense. That is, reason can only take you so far in understanding what's behind your unfinished business. Faith must take you the rest of the way and, when combined with reason, becomes the godly wisdom that allows you to discern the truth that connects what seems to be unrelated.

Wisdom isn't gut instinct. We sometimes admire those who can make snap decisions even when confronted with choices in unfamiliar situations, crediting them with having "gut instinct," an uncanny ability to make the right decision in the midst of the unknown. Pilots might call it "flying by the seat of their pants," and we may have heard someone talk about "navigating by the tip of my nose." It's easy to believe there's a sixth sense that allows us to make decisions without information, and some even pride themselves on it.

And most of those decisions will turn out well because you've been reflecting on those things and applying your knowledge over a period of time. So those quick decisions that seem to come from gut instinct aren't wisdom itself — they're a sign that wisdom is the driving force because what looks like gut instinct is really reliance on the full range of wisdom from critical thinking to assumptions that quickly come together in wise decisions.

Nor is wisdom being an academic high achiever. Although intellectual knowledge is helpful, it can become deadweight if you think you have to know everything before you can make wise decisions. You'll never have perfect knowledge, so your assumptions, those steps of faith you treat as fact fill in the gaps. And if you've examined those assumptions against the objective truth God provides in the Bible, you'll be able to make wise decisions even without perfect information.

You can make effective decisions without perfect information because wisdom gives you the ability to discern the truth of the situation, even in a surprise situation when you don't have time to think. That's because wisdom is more like a habit instead of an effort. It keeps you from double-mindedness.

You may have experienced double-mindedness in different ways. Have you asked others what movie they'd like to see and had them respond by shrugging their shoulders and saying they don't care, what do you want to see? And you shrugged your shoulders in response and replied you don't care either. And it goes back and forth until someone finally ends the impasse by firmly suggesting a movie.

Such double-mindedness shows up in other ways as well — college students trying to decide their majors, dating couples trying to decide whether marriage is the next step, and businesses trying to decide on their next course of action. Sometimes it's called "paralysis by analysis" and is pictured in the Bible as being "like the surf of the sea, driven and tossed by the wind" (James 1:6).

Ironically, a perverted use of wisdom can create problems for people as well. The Bible describes the serpent in Eden as "crafty," a word that can also be translated as "wise." That serpent managed to confuse Eve about God's command not to eat the fruit of a certain tree because it knew which of Eve's buttons to push.

In that exchange, the serpent challenged Eve's understanding of God's command, convincing her that God's command didn't make sense and that her desires were more important. To underscore the irony, Eve saw that the tree "was desirable to make one wise" (Genesis 3:6).

Wise people are therefore more likely to avoid ethical conflicts as well. The ethical problems that befall people are often the result of putting things off to the point where they feel like they have to take shortcuts to catch up, choosing the easier wrong because they didn't take the time earlier for the harder right. I recall a time when I succumbed, frantically making up dates on a fire extinguisher inspection tag the night before a safety audit because I hadn't kept up with the requirement to check the fire extinguisher on a regular basis to make sure it worked.

In fact, some of the shocking cases of corporate accounting fraud in the news are similar but on a larger scale. Reluctance to publish accurate financial information in the hope that sales will improve turns into a willingness to fudge the numbers until the costs of business operations and debt payments become so great that even fraudulent financial statements can't hide the truth.

The writer of the Bible's book of Proverbs, the greatest collection of practical living maxims in one location, exhorts readers to seek wisdom in statements that range from sage advice like, "Make your ear attentive to wisdom" (Proverbs 2:2) to urgent directives like, "Acquire wisdom!" (Proverbs 4:5). How do you do that? The key to wisdom is basing your critical thinking and especially your assumptions upon objective truth. When the writer of Proverbs makes statements like, "the Lord gives wisdom" (Proverbs 2:6), he's telling you what that objective truth is, that the first step is to ground yourself in God to give yourself valid assumptions.

The characteristic of God that should become your priority in this dimension of life, therefore, is the reminder what Jesus Christ said about Himself, that He is "the truth" (John 14:6). This simple and bold declaration anchors your assumptions and is the starting point for critical thinking. Jesus' statement declares that the discernment leading to effective decisions comes from that understanding of who He is because His character and teachings are the objective truth to which you can fasten your thinking and compare arguments made by others.

Adopt some disciplines that will help you increase in wisdom. One of the results will be learning what effective decisions look like. Here are some disciplines you can follow:

- Read. By reflecting on other people's ideas and experiences, you make deposits into your knowledge bank and even give yourself some patterns you might recognize in life situations.

If you surf the Internet, you'll find numerous reading lists from which you can draw ideas for books to read.

- Write. A great thinker of Renaissance England, Francis Bacon, said, "Reading makes a full man; conference a ready man; and writing an exact man." Writing forces you to organize your thoughts in clear ways. But in your busy life, who has time to write? Perhaps it's time to take email seriously. You probably use email extensively in communicating with other people — try writing your emails more formally so you can practice organizing your thoughts and expressing them clearly. For example, instead of just telling friends you had a good weekend, try describing the weekend as if you were writing a short article. Or instead of emailing a link to an article that impressed you to friends with an exclamatory, "This is really good," add some sentences explaining why you thought it was a good article.

- Analyze. Look for the assumptions in arguments. One way to do that might be to read a range of opinions on particular topics so you can see how the writers used facts to support their positions. One place to start would be with the opinions of people you're familiar with. Try to predict what their opinion would be on a particular topic. If you can predict someone's opinion regularly, ask yourself what makes that person's opinions so predictable.

- Listen. Pay attention to people whom you respect. Ask yourself what it is about their thinking that makes you respect them so.

- Learn. Don't hesitate to take formal courses to broaden your view and deepen your understanding. One benefit of formal learning comes from being exposed to knowledge that has already been organized so you can see how it fits together.

Increase in stature to be God's hands and feet

The phrase "Jesus kept increasing in…stature" is set during His adolescence and implies His physical growth into young manhood. Yet, increasing in stature isn't just a matter of getting older and experiencing the change from a child's body to an adult one. It includes gaining knowledge of how to regard your body in terms of your faith.

Your body is an incredible creation, capable of feats of strength and endurance you thought impossible. In a crisis, you can summon reserves of strength you didn't know you had, and you can develop a great amount of endurance with moderate effort. In fact, if you haven't done it yourself, you probably know someone who achieved the goal of running a marathon, even achieving that level of conditioning in about six months to a year.

I've read articles describing how the human body's design for endurance is very different from animals, its skeletal structure and heat exchange system being uniquely suited for endeavors like long distance running. You might not be able to sprint as fast as most animals, but you can run them into the ground. But although your body is a marvelously efficient machine, it needs care so it can achieve peak performance for you and continue performing at a high level during the course of your life.

No, you probably won't be a championship athlete, but performing at peak levels involves achieving a quality of life that helps you pursue your unfinished business. You undoubtedly know what it's like to be in bed with an illness like the flu. You don't get anything done — you just lay there and wallow in your aches and misery. That's what life can become without care of the body. It's better to engage in physical disciplines that keep you healthy than to spend time and money on doctors and treatments to patch you together. And you have to adjust those disciplines to suit the different stages of your life.

The human body has always been seen as more than a collection of bones, muscle, organs, and the skin and sinew holding them together. Recall the account of man's creation in Genesis, how "the Lord God formed man of dust from the ground, and breathed into his nostrils the breath of life" (Genesis 2:7), conveying the idea that the body has an important connection to meaningful existence. That verse in Genesis describes body and spirit as an integrated unit, and its connection to God makes the human body a critical component in a meaningful life.

Even other religions like Buddhism have doctrines about the relationship of the body to spirituality, relating the body to desires and the need to transcend them. So this idea of the body as being more than the purely physical crosses cultures, religions, and philosophies, leading to doctrines and approaches affecting attitudes toward it. Some promote asceticism, the refusal to gratify physical desires like hunger, and others promote hedonism, unhesitatingly gratifying those desires by saying things like "Eat, drink, and be merry, for tomorrow we die."

The ancient Greeks among others proposed a middle way, describing moderation as the key to satisfying physical desires without overdoing it. Aristotle explained what he called the "doctrine of the mean," a middle ground between the extremes at opposite ends. For the body, he would use the word "temperance" to distinguish the mean between profligate behavior like gluttony and self-abusive behavior like anorexia.

Christian thinking also held up the body as special with Paul asking Christians in Corinth, "do you not know that your body is a temple of the Holy Spirit who is in you, whom you have from God, and that you are not your own?" (I Corinthians 6:19). This rhetorical question shows why your body is critical to your unfinished business. While most people acknowledge the importance of taking care of their bodies, they do it so they can enjoy life. After all, who wants to let their bodies get into a condition that limits what they can do? Like the ancient Greeks and others who recognize that treating their bodies at one extreme or the other doesn't have very pleasurable outcomes, most will try to exercise a degree of moderation.

But Paul's question is an illustration that takes moderation a step further and links your body to your unfinished business. Temples are the spots on earth where people meet the supernatural. Sacrifices were offered to gods in ancient temples and people received wisdom from the god or gods they worshipped. People designed and decorated temples to reflect that supernatural environment. Today's church buildings continue that impulse, the great cathedrals of Europe reflecting God's majesty through their soaring architecture and everyday buildings converted to churches reflecting God's intimacy with His believers.

The Jewish temple was the actual dwelling place of God, and Paul used that illustration to stress that God now dwelt in those who worshipped Him. The temple in Jerusalem was the center of religious life, and its design showed worshippers what heaven might look like, the numerous sculptures of cherubim and seraphim reminding the Jews of the heavenly host praising God and its construction materials conveying a sense of heaven's richness. It was the focal point of a religion the God of which called its followers "a kingdom of priests" (Exodus 19:6) to stress why they were a chosen people. God was charging Israel to represent Him to the other nations, an ongoing mission that was their unfinished business as a nation.

And that's why Paul calls your body a temple. It too is where the supernatural God meets the world. He doesn't always perform spectacular signs because He's chosen to serve the world through your hands and feet, see the world's needs with your eyes, and communicate with the world through your mouth. You yourself are the spot on earth where God meets man. Because of that, God has equipped you with your body not as much to pursue pleasure but to pursue your unfinished business. However, enjoying life and experiencing pleasure can be favorable byproducts.

That's because there's a principle of design that declares, "Form follows function," and holds that effective design is the result of supporting the function. So the beauty of a piece of furniture, for example, is less from ornamentation and more from its ability to fulfill its function of providing a spot for rest, storage, dining, or a multitude of other uses. And because the ornamentation supports the design, the object's beauty is all the greater.

Shaker furniture, for example, is popular because those who admire it appreciate how its simple design comes from the simple lifestyle of that religious group. And the original Macintosh computer was elegant in its blending of simplicity and functionality that resulted in a sleek look.

Your body follows the same principle, its form supporting your unfinished business because you have physical attributes that make you more suited for some pursuits than others. You might be an Eric Liddell whose running speed propelled him to the 1924 Olympics and gave him a platform for speaking about his faith to others. Or you might be like Mother Teresa, whose frail looking stature underscored the compassion behind her work with the poor in Calcutta.

But form and function go beyond appearance and athleticism. Dealing with physical affliction might become part of your unfinished business. When I was younger, I heard about Joni Eareckson Tada, wheelchair bound after a diving accident, who turned her disability into a platform for explaining God's ways to people and advocating for the disabled. Today, her work is globally recognized and powerfully shows how God meets the world through her body. You too can turn what seems like a fractured form that could not possibly be of use in this world into a vessel of inspiration and accomplishment, a catalyst launching you toward your unfinished business.

Your physical state changes with the various stages of life. In your younger years, you can take on vigorous projects, some of which might be very adventurous, because you have strength, endurance, and the ability to heal quickly. That last quality isn't trivial. Athletes pursue their careers successfully because their youth enables them to withstand and even thrive under the physical demands of season long competition. And young professionals like doctors and lawyers endure grueling schedules that would break older constitutions.

As you age, you temper your activity to account for changes in your physical make-up. You're more deliberate in what you do and rely more on the wisdom of experience to help you be more efficient in your activities. Besides the natural physical changes you experience, your care in managing your activities might also come from the hard effort of your younger years catching up to you. Several of my friends are military veterans who served in elite units. The extreme levels of physical activity took its toll on their bodies, causing the early appearance of arthritis and other joint ailments similar to what many professional athletes experience in their later years.

Increasing in stature is therefore not just about physical appearance. When God was looking for someone to replace Saul as Israel's king, He reminded His prophet Samuel that "God sees not as man sees, for man looks at the outward appearance, but the Lord looks at the heart" (I Samuel 16:7). Saul had looked like a king, being a head taller than most men in Israel. Yet he made bad decisions and forfeited the kingdom.

When God picked David to replace Saul, God picked someone who was the youngest male of an insignificant family. David's father even forgot about him when Samuel came to their home. After meeting seven of Jesse's sons, Samuel had to remind Jesse there was an eighth son to meet. So what you do with your body isn't about looking good or making an impression, it's about harnessing your physical make-up to a purpose.

It also means your body is a record of your life experiences, decisions and incidents that show up in your body in different ways. Oscar Wilde wrote *The Picture of Dorian Gray*, a novel about a young man whose painted portrait changed to reflect the results of a depraved life while he himself remained as youthful and handsome as ever.

In a similar way, your body reflects your life experiences as well as what you think is important. My father for example stressed safety with tools, his stubby right thumb a permanent reminder of a lawnmower accident in his younger years.

The degree to which you exercise, the risks you take in your physical activities, the things you put into your body all show up in your physical makeup, with even your body language reflecting what's on your mind. Remember how you wouldn't look your parents in the eye when they caught you doing something wrong and asked you to admit it? You shuffled around and looked everywhere else. And you remember their advice to you to stand straight with shoulders back and chest out because your posture radiates your degree of self-confidence. Your words may convey one thing, but your body never lies.

Harnessing your body to a purpose rather than just enjoying life can also bolster your courage. The Founding Fathers of the United States risked execution as traitors because they believed their purpose was greater than their lives, and Ronald Reagan, knowing his life was subordinate to a greater cause, was able to quip to his wife after being shot, "I forgot to duck."

That courage can also take the form of self-sacrifice. One of my favorite stories is about Philip Sydney, the archetypal Renaissance man in Queen Elizabeth's court who was famous as a poet, statesman, and soldier in sixteenth century England. While being treated for a wound from which he was to later die, Sydney passed his ration of water to another wounded soldier, saying, "Thy need is greater than mine."

Treating your body as a temple therefore means developing it to help you pursue your unfinished business. This means undertaking some physical disciplines that help you grow beyond your appetites. Otherwise, your priorities will be self-focused, seeking gratification instead of fulfilling a purpose.

While there may be nothing inherently wrong with seeking pleasure, making it a goal will prove unsatisfying because pleasure, being temporary, will put you on a treadmill of seeking the next pleasurable thing.

Therefore, the characteristic of God on which to build your priorities comes from Jesus' reminder to the Samaritan woman, "God is spirit" (John 4:24), in response to her mentioning a difference between Jews and Samaritans. Jews worshipped in Jerusalem and Samaritans at Mount Gerizim in Samaria. If God is spirit, according to Jesus, then worship is an attitude of the heart, not a method of presentation.

So in responding to her comment about where to go to properly worship God, Jesus assured her she could encounter God anywhere, not just through a pilgrimage to a holy place. And from that encounter, other Samaritans in that city heeded Jesus' teachings and became God's friends, something that wouldn't have been possible if He had not gone out to them.

In a sense, therefore, we make it possible for people to encounter God where they are in life if we treat our bodies as temples. Rather than expecting people to go to a prescribed location to find God, we can bring God to them because God is spirit who makes Himself available to people through us as we pursue our unfinished business. Here are some ideas about physical disciplines to pursue:

- Diet is the foundation of your physical disciplines. More than any other physical discipline, diet reflects the connection between your priorities and your actions. That's because food tastes so good, and it seems the food that tastes best is the food that's worst for you. At least it seems that way to this fan of Girl Scout cookies.
- Diet is where you'll most vividly experience the conflict between desire and purpose. Computer programmers have a phrase, "Garbage in, garbage out." They know that computers will do exactly what the program and inputs tell them to do, so programmers make sure the program works as

it should and the inputs are correct. Your body is like a computer in that regard, responding to what you put in it.

- Exercise also is an arena in which the conflict between desire and purpose plays out. Only this time, it's because physical effort isn't so fun, so you may have to push yourself to exercise. As W.C. Fields once said, "Whenever I get the urge to exercise, I lie down until it goes away." It's so much easier to watch television than it is to exercise.

- Rest is the neglected discipline. You'd think everyone would be delighted to engage in this physical discipline, but in a competitive world, the demands of family and career usually trump the need for rest. Doctors say you need seven to eight hours of sleep to recover from the day's activities and prepare for the next. And you have to get your rest consistently. Sleeping is like putting money in the bank, and going without sleep is like taking money out. After a while of going on less sleep than you need, you run out.

- Developing your nonverbal vocabulary is a physical discipline we don't always think about. The reason you can often communicate quickly and efficiently when you're face to face with others is because the nonverbal cues you give off fill in the gaps. A quip with a warm smile signals affection but is biting sarcasm when you make the smile colder. Looking others in the eye implies attention to them, but looking away frequently communicates lack of interest. Your body therefore can convey signals you may or may not intend and affect people's understanding of the message you want to communicate.

Favor positions you for impact

When becoming God's friend launches you on the character-shaping adventure that allows you to boast in what God did, it also gives you a purpose for developing your intellectual and physical capacities. But it doesn't stop there. You have to use that character and capacity to pursue your unfinished business. And that means connecting with others in the spiritual and social dimensions.

That verse in Luke's gospel points out that Jesus increased in favor with God and man. Favor is enhanced standing in someone else's eyes, a position of leverage you can exercise in God's service and for the benefit of others. Think about shifting your body around to get the best position for lifting a heavy piece of furniture or watching sumo wrestlers try to jostle each other out of the ring. In both cases, getting control of the center of gravity is the key to success. Favor puts you in that position.

You gain enhanced standing in someone else's eyes because of the personal credibility that comes from relationships based on integrity. When you demonstrate the fruits of the Spirit over time, follow through with your commitment to disciplines in the life dimensions, partner with God in your development, and seek the counsel of teachers and mentors, your credibility grows because your actions that grow out of those commitments validate your character to others. And that credibility is the currency that purchases favor.

But there is also another way to increase in favor. My wife comes from a Southern family and a phrase they used was "He favors his father" or "She favors her mother." But in this case, it wasn't about enhanced standing; it was about looking like someone else. In the southern United States, the word "favor" is sometimes used to point out the resemblance of one to another. In this sense, you can grow in favor with God when you start to look like Him, that is, when fruits of the Spirit like love, joy, and patience in your life become apparent to others.

Increasing in favor with God, that is, looking like Him, makes sense as a goal of growth, but what about looking like humans? I'm sure you wouldn't mind looking like your favorite beautiful celebrities (an executive assistant told me I needed to get my photo taken for an ID, so I emailed her a photo of Tom Cruise and asked, "Will this do?" She shook her head sadly and responded, "You have some work to do."), but in the sense of resemblance, you can grow in favor with man when others see you becoming more fully human. Paradoxically, that means they'll see more of God in you because you were created in God's image, the state to which He restored you when you became His friend and began pursuing your unfinished business.

Think about people you've met over the years: you hit it off instantly with some, feeling like you've known them forever even if you just met for the first time. Remember that person with whom you fell in love? Even if you hadn't known each other long, something between the two of you kept you talking all night, and you both felt like it wasn't long enough. You found favor with each other because you saw compatible inner character evidenced in outward words and actions.

You find favor, therefore, because you're examined in stages, each stage more exacting until you're transparent, putting you in a position where you're regarded at face value. What others see is what they get. It's like the gradual opening to each other among friends as they get to know each other better.

It's also similar to increasing your responsibilities in other pursuits, beginning with simple things and graduating to greater responsibilities. Your experience is replete with similar examples. In school, you move from simpler subjects to more difficult subjects, and at work, you're entrusted with more to do based on what you did before.

Increasing in favor works the same way. When your words and actions are consistent with each other and with values to which you're committed at a basic level, you're then expected to show that same consistency at higher and more challenging levels. Otherwise, you're branded as a hypocrite and disregarded.

Consistency of words and actions with each other and with values to which you're committed can be rigorous. There is the basic consistency accepted across most cultures that includes values like the universal prohibition against theft and murder and the dream of freedom and equality, values that create community. Your words and actions should be consistent not only with each other but with those universal values.

The environment in which you typically live and operate is the next stage at which you're examined. For example, you may be an employee in a business, a volunteer in a non-profit organization, or member of a formal association of homeowners. Each group has a specific purpose, and the values adopted by that group support what that group wants to accomplish. Similar to creating community, the values are a glue that bond the group members and guide them in acting in ways that help the group achieve its goals. As an employee, you do things to help the company turn a profit, and as a homeowner, you care for your property in ways that enhance the beauty and value of your neighborhood.

But the final stage is where you truly increase in favor, others seeing that your own values, the set by which you have chosen to live, are more stringent and positive than those of the group and of the world at large. At this stage, you have to be seen as holding yourself to higher standards. This is the extra mile philosophy.

In His magnificent Sermon on the Mount, Jesus laid out the concept of having a personal code more stringent than that of the group or world at large, telling His listeners if someone forced them to walk a mile, volunteer to go an extra mile. Scholars have pointed out that Roman soldiers could compel the inhabitants of the occupied land to carry the soldiers' gear for one mile. Jesus preached higher standards: go an extra mile to demonstrate commitment to a higher standard.

But favor isn't preferential treatment of you at the expense of others nor is it preferential treatment by you of others. For example, if a police officer pulled you over for speeding, you can't expect favor to be shown you. You were violating a law and could have jeopardized other people if you lost control of your car. If the police officer lets you off with a warning, be grateful, but don't presume you found favor in his or her eyes. You did something meriting a traffic ticket and fine, so you should consider the warning a lesson, not a license to speed.

Nor is it for the purpose of mutual back scratching. You've no doubt heard the phrase, "You scratch my back, and I'll scratch yours," which implies a relationship of obligation. When you do something for someone else, everyone involved understands you can "call in a favor" or "cash in your chips" when you need help from that person. However, increasing in favor operates according to a paradox — you aren't trying to create a sense of obligation in others. You're simply trying to live a life of integrity without expectation of reward. Increasing in favor is the byproduct of living that life of integrity.

And having favor isn't permanent. It's easy to lose favor by being inconsistent with the values to which you're committed. Think of public figures whose private actions were found to be wildly out of synch with their public image, especially if that public image was a carefully cultivated image of virtue. That for which they worked so hard crashed.

Increasing in favor puts you in a position that multiplies the effectiveness of your abilities and enables you to accomplish more than you thought possible. You not only gain support for what you want to do because of the credibility you've built, you become known for your credibility, and favor seeks you even more, gaining greater access to resources as well as ability to persuade. And you weren't even consciously looking for those results. Ultimately, that growth in influence can have ripples of impact that spread beyond your immediate situation.

Esther became the Persian king's favorite wife, a position of favor and credibility among the members of the king's harem. A Jewish girl living in an era after the Jews had been scattered by conquest, she played a pivotal role in preserving her people. Becoming privy to a plot of genocide against the Jews by one of Persia's high officials, Esther debated bringing it to the king's attention because she hadn't been summoned to the court. In that ancient kingdom, to enter the king's presence without being summoned was a capital offense.

But confronted by her uncle's question, "And who knows whether you have not attained royalty for such a time as this?" (Esther 4:14), Esther steeled herself and went forward unsummoned. And the king responded because of her credibility, his support making it possible for the Jews to defend themselves against this plot and preserve their existence as a distinct people even though spread throughout the Persian Empire.

But Esther's impact has broader ramifications. Remember that Israel suffered those conquests because the nation continually drifted from God to idolatry. During that time of dispersal, the Jews developed two great institutions to preserve their distinctive identity and cleave more closely to God. Instead of traveling to Jerusalem to worship, they began meeting locally, creating synagogues where they worshipped. In addition to worship based in local communities, they emphasized Scripture reading in those worship services, an act that preserved their doctrines in spite of geographic separation.

Those institutions now show up in Christianity as Christians meet locally to worship and also ground their faith in the Bible's words. An act of influence therefore not only helped the Jews survive in ancient Persia, it preserved a pair of institutions that helped Christians grow their faith first throughout the Roman Empire and then around the world. That's because a faith that wasn't anchored to a specific location was portable. But it could stay firm and consistent because Christians read from the same text no matter where they lived. You too can have broad and lasting influence.

So because you're positioned for greater impact, you'll have the opportunity to accomplish a greater good. Because your experience in all the areas of your life gave you an understanding of your place in this world, you'll know how to use the leverage that favor has given you.

And notice it positions you to fulfill the two great commandments because increasing in favor with God and man corresponds symmetrically with Jesus' point that the whole of the law, that is, the body of Jewish law symbolized by the Ten Commandments, boils down to two principles: love God and love your neighbor. It therefore demonstrates how God's priorities are becoming your priorities (something He has been doing in your life since you became His friend) and preparing you to become His blessing to other people.

Although favor is enhanced standing in another's eyes giving you leverage you can exercise in God's service and for the benefit of others, you can prepare yourself to take advantage of that better position. By equipping yourself to live by a higher standard, you not only enhance the credibility you need to increase in favor, you give yourself tools to take advantage of that better position. To acquire those tools, Paul encouraged Christians in Ephesus to:

> Put on the full armor of God, so that you will be able to stand firm against the schemes of the devil. For our struggle is not against flesh and blood, but against the rulers, against the powers, against the world forces of this darkness, against the spiritual forces of wickedness in the heavenly places. Therefore, take up the full armor of God, so that you will be able to resist in the evil day, and having done everything, to stand firm. Stand firm therefore, having girded your loins with truth, and having put on the breastplate of righteousness, and having shod your feet with the preparation of the gospel of peace; in addition to all, taking up the shield of faith with which you will be able to extinguish all the flaming arrows of the evil one. And take the helmet of salvation, and the sword of the Spirit, which is the word of God. (Ephesians 6:11-17)

The realm in which values exist, according to Paul, is an environment above flesh and blood, a spiritual arena of influences, purposes, and motives. It's a complex place where you need to position yourself on something firm. Because you can't read other people's minds to know if you have the degree of credibility that gives you favor in their eyes, you have to adopt practices that have passed the test of time, ways of living shown through the ages to be more exacting than those of the world at large. You have to live virtuously, and the full armor of God gives you the way to live that life.

First, Paul makes this admonition in his letter after listing practical ways to build the kind of credibility that leads to favor. From creating strong marriages to effective parenting to work relationships discussed earlier in the letter, Paul charged his readers in Ephesus to live wisely because the reality of the world was one which transcended flesh and blood. It would be an easy thing if existence was purely material, if flesh and blood was all there was. If what mattered was only what could be seen, touched, heard, smelled, and tasted, life would be much simpler, Paul's readers could instead concentrate on doing what pleased them or what met their desires.

In first century Ephesus, it would therefore make sense, for example, for masters to treat their slaves harshly — it makes sense to extract as much work as possible from slaves because they were a fixed investment. Slave owners not only had spent money initially to buy their slaves, they had to provide the ongoing upkeep of food, clothing, and shelter for the slaves. Forcing extra work from slaves gave owners more value for their investment. And it would make sense for men to demand that large dowries come with their wives to help establish the new estate or improve the prospects of an inherited one.

But there's more at stake than flesh and blood. Paul understood that the physical world is merely a stage where greater things are accomplished. The rulers, powers, world forces, and spiritual forces he listed are behind the influences, aspirations, and intentions that motivate human actions and

possibly keep people from making their words and actions fully consistent with each other and with their stated values.

For example, capitalizing on the citizens' belief that the goddess Diana had particularly blessed Ephesus, the business people of Ephesus had created a prosperous trade in silver idols that became an important part of the city's economy. They became violent when Paul's progress in converting the city dwellers to Christianity threatened that revenue source. The need for income to feed their families had become a desire for wealth they were willing to protect at all costs.

So Paul prescribed an approach to help his readers live in ways that would enhance their standing as virtuous people and give them the credibility that increases favor. Putting on the armor of God would equip them to be consistent. The qualities of truth, righteousness, peace, faith, and salvation are the foundation from which virtuous living grows. They establish that higher standard to which Paul's readers could aspire and still support values that help build community. And the word of God, what we today call the Bible, provides the knowledge about those qualities that undergird the disciplines you willingly undertake, so you can use the circumstances God allows into your life to convert that knowledge into godly habit.

Increase in favor with God to become an example

Favor with God is an enhanced standing in God's eyes that positions you to be a conduit through which God can bless the world. That's the special leverage you have with Him. The greatest example occurred when the angel Gabriel said to a young woman, "Greetings, favored one! The Lord is with you" (Luke 1:28) and told her about a child she would bear even though she was not married. Because Mary had found favor with God, she was the vessel through whom God blessed the world by becoming Jesus Christ's mother.

Your having God's favor will make you a similar vessel through whom God will bless those around you. It may become a spectacular ministry like Billy Graham's evangelistic crusades or involve sharing a quiet coffee with a neighbor. It may become a great social achievement like William Wilberforce's work in persuading Great Britain to end slavery or it may be a few well chosen words that bring clarity to how a friend responds to an upcoming surgery.

Those who are such vessels are called holy. Reference works point out that the Greek word from which "holy" comes, *hagios*, means "set apart." These are people who have been set apart for a purpose. Paul called holy those to whom he addressed his letters, telling his readers they had a certain destiny and charging them to live in a manner worthy of that destiny. His charge to "present your bodies a living and holy sacrifice, acceptable to God, which is your spiritual service of worship" (Romans 12:1) uses the word "living" to paint a picture of an ongoing process, a way of life he wanted his readers to adopt because they were now special.

Have you been told you were special? Perhaps someone took you under his or her wing and said you had the potential to do great things. A teacher may have given you a little extra work to bring out that potential. It may have been an indication you had the potential to go farther in school or athletics.

Perhaps you were encouraged to join an honor society or a special section of the school band. Many high school bands have groups specializing in musical genres like jazz that meet at times other than regular practice for additional work in their specialty. They've been set apart for a purpose. When you have God's favor, He's telling you that you're not only special, you have a special mission, one that will require more from you and bring out the greatness in you.

My dad had a terrific workshop in his garage stocked with power tools and specialty equipment he collected over the years. He was loath to use a tool for other than its intended purpose, taking the time, for example, to go back and get a small crowbar for prying instead of using a screwdriver lying next to him. He knew that prying something with a screwdriver could damage the tip and make the screwdriver useless for its real purpose of driving screws. When you have God's favor, you're like a tool set aside for a specific purpose and cared for so you can fulfill that purpose effectively.

Increasing in favor with God teaches you how to integrate your deepening friendship with Him into your spiritual life. If you're like me, you may be used to approaching God when you need something instead of approaching Him for the sake of being with Him. How long would a relationship between humans last if they approached each other that way?

Can you imagine a husband and wife not enjoying each other's company but treating their relationship like a business transaction? Businesses won't hesitate to tell their contractual partners they want to renegotiate the contract if the cost gets too high. And if the benefits of a new contract outweigh the penalty of breaking the current contract outright, so be it. Interpersonal relationships can't exist that way, and your relationship with God is no different.

Moses understood that. If anyone had a right to approach God on a needs-based relationship, it was Moses. Here was a shy man with a speech impediment thrust into a confrontation with the leader of a superpower, telling Pharaoh to free the Hebrews from their slave status in Egypt. That's like telling a modern nation to give up a core portion of its economy, for example, telling modern China to give up its manufacturing capability or the United States to give up its high technology and entertainment industries. Moses had been set apart for the specific purpose of bringing the Hebrews out of Egypt, first called when he heard God's voice and later prepared when God explained His mission.

Moses went from being responsible for a family and a flock of sheep to leading hundreds of thousands of people on a journey through unfamiliar territory while being chased by an army. And if that wasn't enough, he had, as it turned out, only forty years to take this mob with no institutions around which they could build a society and turn them into a functioning, cohesive nation with an identity that distinguished them from the surrounding nations.

So what did he ask God for? Did he ask God for a vaulting intellect with which to solve national problems for which there was no precedent? Did he ask God for irresistible charisma with which he could persuade the people to accept difficult courses of action? Did he ask God for national treasure upon which he could build a thriving economy? No. Instead, he asked, "if I have found favor in Your sight, let me know Your ways that I may know You" (Exodus 33:13). Moses' concern was with representing God well because he understood that solutions to all those other concerns would flow from that foundation.

Moses did all that on Mount Sinai when God was telling him the laws that would govern the new nation. That time on Mount Sinai was so intense Moses' face shone, a phenomenon so unique and obvious it frightened the Israelites for a while. That's what encounters with God do to people. Those who decide to give priority to a relationship with God by taking on disciplines like developing relationships with like-minded people and approaching God through prayer and reading the Bible become similarly marked. There's something about people's demeanor, words, and actions that seems different. That's because those activities turn their knowledge into habit by changing their focus to substantive and inner things, a condition called conformity to Christ.

Increasing in favor with God doesn't mean you have to become legalistic or ascetic. You don't have to follow a strict set of procedures or deny yourself excessively. These approaches imply you expect God to give you special treatment because you did things a certain way. While it might make sense to do those things in certain situations, it's easy to fall into the trap of doing them to get a reward instead of building a relationship.

It's also tempting to think denying yourself all pleasure is the right path. After all, it could have been the consequences of seeking pleasure that made you realize you needed to change your priorities. But emphasizing what you shouldn't be doing only puts those very things in front of you as temptations. I heard a comedian say it this way: "The Bible is full of so many things to do, that if you're doing the do's, you won't have time to do the don'ts!"

Because favor is an enhanced standing in the eyes of others, you have leverage. In a way, increasing in favor with God gives you leverage with God. When God was ready to wipe out Sodom and Gomorrah, Abraham talked Him into withholding that destruction if only ten righteous people could be found in those cities. And Abraham may even have been able to convince God to spare the cities completely if he had just asked. That's because leverage with God isn't the same thing we typically understand it to be.

If you have leverage with someone, you can persuade that person to do something in line with what you want. Like using a fulcrum and lever to move heavy things out of the way, favor with others means you have sources to help you get things done you couldn't do by yourself. *But leverage with God is different. Instead of getting help in moving things out of the way, you're giving God the lever and fulcrum to move you out of the way.* In other words, you're giving Him the control of your life so He can use you for His purposes.

As you'll read in the next section, giving God the lever and fulcrum, that is, control over your life, ultimately allows Him to turn you into the lever and fulcrum He'll use to move others. In Abraham's case, it wasn't that Abraham persuaded God to change His mind — it was that Abraham, in that request for mercy, showed he had advanced another step toward God's ultimate goal for him: to become the father of a nation, to become the lever and fulcrum with which God would bless the world.

To increase in favor with God, take on His goodness. Jesus declared that part of God's character when He told the rich young ruler, "No one is good except God" (Luke 18:19). If that's the case, how can we be good enough to the point of becoming set apart as examples? It's the striving that will set you apart. The simple act of striving after goodness is enough to set you apart from the common endeavors of life and reminds me of a sentiment from West Point's Cadet Prayer shared by many, "Make us to choose the harder right instead of the easier wrong." But how?

Obedience to God is the strategic quality you need to increase in favor with Him, and Jesus Christ is both your teacher and great example, going farther than any of us would dream of going because "He humbled Himself by becoming obedient to the point of death, even death on a cross" (Philippians 2:8). He set an example by forgoing the privileges of His standing as Son of God and accepting pain and rejection as Son of Man.

Obedience usually involves a willingness to set your desires aside for a greater goal, a quality strengthened by your response to circumstances that come your way as you pursue your unfinished business. It's also a way of life, a set of habits you can develop by taking up several disciplines you've probably heard about.

- Prayer is your foundational discipline that ingrains obedience into your character. The simple act of becoming consistent in prayer is the first step toward obedience. Here are several ideas on how to achieve that consistency:
  - Commit some time during the day, even if it's a short amount. In this sense, prayer is like exercise — as you develop your conditioning, you'll do more.
  - Take up some tools to help you pray. A devotional book with short readings is a superb tool that helps you achieve consistency. It's always there, ready for your use.

- A journal in which you at least list prayer items helps you pray from your heart. Don't worry if your prayer items seem like favor-seeking at first, a chronicle of asking for this and that. You have to begin where you're at in life. As you become more aligned to what God wants, your prayer items will become more substantive.

- Bible reading is another fundamental discipline. Developing consistency in this discipline will also ingrain obedience into your character. Reading the Bible not only exposes you to deep truths, it also expands your intellect.

  - You can read sections at a time, often getting reading plans from web sites on the Internet or from your own Bible. Usually, one chapter at a time helps you digest the knowledge at a reasonable rate.

  - When I first began reading the Bible, I found that reading the Gospels and Acts first, and then the histories in the Old Testament was a useful sequence. The New Testament books helped put the Old Testament into context because of the references Jesus and the apostles made to the Old Testament. And the narratives were much more interesting than tabulations of numbers, genealogies, and laws found in other parts of the Bible.

- Keeping the Sabbath, that is, attending church regularly, keeps you in touch with like-minded people. A burning coal left by itself quickly dies out but helps create much heat when part of the pile. You need the strength that community brings, and church is where you find that community. This discipline also challenges you to take time away from yourself and give it to God because it's on the weekend, an exercise in obedience because of the competing attractions.

  - If you're looking for a church, take its doctrinal stance seriously. Ask to read their doctrinal statements and match them with your reading of the Bible. One way to examine their doctrinal stance is to compare it with the great Christian creeds like the Nicene Creed or the

Apostle's Creed. These are straightforward statements of Christian belief that were created centuries ago to clarify what Christians believed. You can easily find them on the Internet or in books at your local library. Just remember that the phrase "catholic church" in those creeds refers to the universal church, hence the small "c" to emphasize the unity of all Christians.

o   If you visit a church for the first time, don't feel slighted if people don't flock to welcome you. They may be just as shy about meeting strangers as you probably are. While some congregations may have lapsed into cold exclusivity and lack of hospitality, keep in mind that people aren't perfect. I've heard some say after visiting a church only once that they didn't like it because no one came up to shake hands and welcome them. Could it be that expecting members of a church to be perfectly welcoming is like expecting patients in a hospital to jump up and play a round of basketball? People go to church because they're spiritually broken and need God to put them back together. So when you visit a church, remember you're a broken person seeing other broken people who may still be responding in broken ways.

o   When you join a church, get active. Don't just be a pew-warmer — get involved. In sports, being a bench-warmer means not getting in the game. But isn't playing the game the reason to get involved in a sport? Going to church is the same thing. Do something. Churches are crying for volunteers, and God has given you certain gifts to use in the service of others. Of course, don't overdo it. Maintain balance by remembering this little rhyme I heard long ago: "Mary had a little lamb, / It never became a sheep. / It got involved in all the programs / And died from lack of sleep."

• Take up the discipline of tithing. This is perhaps the most uncomfortable discipline of them all. After all, this is money we're talking about, and there are many pressing things seeking to separate us from our money. Or is it our money? Giving a portion of our money to God reveals the true alignment of our priorities because it means giving up a portion we could spend today or invest in the future. We think it therefore makes our stay in this world a little less comfortable, but that may be the point. When we're less comfortable about our place in this world, we have to seek comfort in God.

Increase in favor with man to gain opportunities to serve

Increasing in favor with God may set you apart because the obedience you exercise aligns you with God's goodness, but what do you do about it? Everything to this point has been about taking on priorities that give you a way to look at the world and see its needs from God's perspective, creating a burden for meeting those needs.

But one more area of priorities is the tipping point, increasing that burden to where it overflows into action. That area is to increase in favor with man. Increasing in favor with man is when you learn how to integrate faith into the social dimension, turning your faith into concrete and practical actions to give you an enhanced standing in other people's eyes.

You begin to increase in favor with man because those inner changes make you more fully human. Paradoxically, becoming more fully human is the inevitable result of increasing in favor with God, a process I like to call a virtuous circle. Remember that God "created man in His own image, in the image of God He created him; male and female He created them" (Genesis 1:27). God made you to look like Him, and when you break with that relationship, you drift away from that image, making it harder for others to see God in you.

Where increasing in favor with God was like a tool being set aside for a specific purpose, increasing in favor with man is like a tool being used for its purpose. Watch a car race and you know those automobiles were made for speed: the family car wouldn't fit. And when those racing cars flash past doing what they're supposed to do, they're a magnificent sight. But they'd be woefully out of place on a major city's gridlocked highways. Likewise, the U.S. Navy's Blue Angels and U.S. Air Force's Thunderbirds fly high performance jets that enable them to perform stomach-dropping aerial maneuvers, functions for which the planes were designed that leave spectators slack-jawed with amazement.

Becoming more fully human therefore means God will begin using you according the purpose for which He designed you, turning you into the lever and fulcrum you read about in the last section. This time, however, it's to move others. That's because the qualities you display help earn the right to be heard by others and open them to your service.

When Jesus acknowledged Peter's confessing that Jesus was the Christ, the anointed one whom God sent, He said of Peter's statement, "…upon this rock I will build My church; and the gates of Hades will not overpower it" (Matthew 16:18). That's what being turned into a fulcrum and lever means — you're the tool by which God will open those gates enclosing people's hearts.

Christianity grew in ancient Rome in spite of persecution because those who watched Christians saw God's image. They saw characteristics like integrity and love played out every day in the lives of those ancient Christians. And it's growing around the world today. One of the little told stories is the explosive growth of Christianity in the developing world, especially in countries hostile to the Gospel.

The Roman emperor Julian, who tried to restore paganism to its previous prominence, was concerned that the conduct of Christians was hindering his success, writing about them, "Why then do we think that this is sufficient and do not observe how the kindness of Christians to strangers, their care for the burial of their dead, and the sobriety of their lifestyle has done the most to advance their cause?" That evidence of behavior helps you earn the right to be heard by others.

You also earn the right to be heard because of the diligence you display when you follow Jesus' example in setting your priorities as well as increasing in wisdom and stature and in favor with God. That doesn't mean you have to be a star or achieve perfect results. It means you have to be serious about what you do. Students should be diligent with their studies. Full-time homemakers should be diligent at creating environments for supportive and encouraging relationships. And workers should be focused on giving their employers and customers an honest day's work.

That's because you're not doing those things for yourself or even for others; instead, "whatever you do, do all to the glory of God" (I Corinthians 10:31). Notice how the focus on God, on looking like His image, makes you more effective in what you do and therefore more credible in the eyes of others. After all, who would take God seriously whose followers surfed the Internet all day at work or allowed their homes to fall into disrepair through lack of care?

But increasing in favor with man isn't a popularity contest. Favor with man isn't a matter of how much others like you, although it can be useful in communicating God's love to them. There will be times when you'll have to take a stand or at least point out an unpleasant truth. While there may be consequences you won't like, it will keep your credibility intact.

That's what favor with man is, credibility that earns you the right to be heard. It's the contrast between Pontius Pilate and Jesus — Jesus remained true to His mission while Pilate, even though finding no guilt in Jesus, sentenced Jesus to death to placate those who agitated against Him. The Jewish leaders wanted Jesus dead but needed a conviction under Roman law to trigger capital punishment. So they took Jesus' words like, "My kingdom," spiced them up with stories from false witnesses, and presented Jesus to Pilate as a seditionist.

For Pilate, this was a quandary. He quickly saw through their ploy but must have understood that if his superiors heard he released someone claiming to be a king...well, that could be hard to explain. So he tried another tack: let the people decide. But the Jewish leaders were ready when Pilate proposed a public choice of prisoners for release, inciting the crowd to near riot in favor of Barabbas, a known criminal.

Outsmarted at every turn, Pilate ultimately had Jesus executed rather than allow himself to be portrayed as a weak administrator. Even the famous scene in which he washed his hands to symbolize his disassociation with the whole affair has done nothing to lessen his responsibility in the eyes of history. So Pilate, thinking he was fulfilling his mission as an administrator of keeping order in the territory, ended up failing in his mission. Such things happen when the birds of expediency come home to roost.

Nor is increasing in favor with man something you can achieve immediately. Earning the right to be heard takes time and doesn't yield to those who are impatient and want to see results immediately. Think about how you reacted to a sales representative whom you met for the first time but who talked to you as if a long time friend. You didn't fall for it. Increasing in favor with man operates the same way. You can't hope to have credibility right away because those whom you know best you trust most.

The end of all that relationship building is the opportunity to serve others because your efforts at building credibility make them more likely to accept your service — you won't come across as that sales representative who has a hidden agenda. Increasing in favor with man puts you in an enhanced position that allows you to serve others. That service can take the form of good works, pulling together resources to help those in need. For example, Christian relief organizations are credible because only a small portion of the donations goes to overhead.

Donors are confident their money will be used for its intended purpose.

Increasing in favor with man also transforms your place in society. Remember that whatever you do should be done to the glory of God. That means your motives are no longer *self*-directed: they're *God*-directed, giving you a stronger platform from which to communicate who God is to those around you.

Let's take a controversial topic: Paul's statement to wives to "be subject to your own husbands, as to the Lord" (Ephesians 5:22). In today's society, that sets a lot of people's teeth on edge. Yet, in the context of the ancient world, it was a radical transformation of the marriage relationship.

Because marriages were arranged, it wasn't uncommon, especially in the upper classes, for wives to look elsewhere for romance and treat the marriage relationship with some cynicism. After all, they were lower in the pecking order. But Paul charged women to take a different approach. By bringing their wifely role under the rubric of a relationship with God, women would be able to impact their husbands' lives so "they may be won without a word by the behavior of their wives" (I Peter 3:1).

And husbands weren't off the hook either. In the ancient world as well as parts of the modern world, men were entitled to expect a dowry from their bride's family. This and other customs gave men primacy in the marriage relationship. So Paul wanted men to be radical as well, charging his male readers to "love your wives, just as Christ also loved the church and gave Himself up for her" (Ephesians 5:25). In effect, he was asking men to give up their positions of privilege just as Christ gave up His position in heaven to sleep in a feeding trough, wash people's feet, and die a criminal's death.

I've heard men say Paul's statement means that just as Christ died for the church, husbands should be willing to die for their wives, evoking the magnificent spirit of the men of the *Titanic* who said, "Women and children first." While I agree that statement defines a man's code, I think Paul expected men to *live* for their wives as well. That means a lifetime serving their ladies just as Christ served His followers.

Gaining the credibility that earns you the right to serve sounds very pragmatic, and that's because it is. But it happens because you don't live in a pragmatic way. The changes in your behavior attract attention because, strangely enough, the priority in this dimension of your life doesn't seek attention. That aspect of God's character you take as your priority in this dimension is humility.

When Jesus said, "I...am humble" (Matthew 11:29), He pointed to Himself as an example. And because the apostle John tells us Jesus explained God, that statement reveals humility as a part of God's character to take on. So it's humility that tips the scales to make the changes inside you apparent to others.

It's a non-pragmatic approach with a pragmatic outcome because humility is not a widely accepted virtue in this world. Instead of being self-serving, it's self-effacing to the degree that your own desires disappear and others' needs take precedence. Humility allows you to seek what's best *for* others, even enemies and untouchables, by giving your best *to* others and seeking nothing in return. And the result is a very practical kind of credibility that directs people's attention to the God who inspired it. When Mother Teresa spoke, for example, people listened.

Humility shows up in the small things. I heard a humorous comment that has a lot of truth to it: "Everybody wants to save the world, but no one helps Mom with the dishes." Humility calls us to set our own agendas aside and take a few minutes to help Mom. Those small things are important because they reveal the foundation on which you build your character.

Humility is foundational because it's nothing more than an accurate assessment of your capabilities and entitlements as seen through God's eyes. That accurate assessment therefore helps us seek what's best for others because it teaches us the truth in the saying, "There but for the grace of God go I." There are a number of practical disciplines that help develop and reinforce humility.

The discipline making that assessment possible is integrity. I recall movie epics about the ancient world showing the warriors saluting by striking their armor breastplates over their hearts with their right fists and found an explanation that described it as a way to show they were ready for battle. Striking their armor over their hearts showed it was firmly attached over the most vulnerable part of their bodies. Your character has to hold together like that.

Integrity demonstrates love of others because it makes you transparent. They don't have to be on their guard around you. It's a tool that helps you achieve humility because the strength of your integrity is a standard against which you can evaluate your character development. There are several approaches to strengthening your integrity.

- Be prepared to lose. In practical terms, that means things like having an emergency fund in the bank in case you get laid off as well as understanding that money you may have invested in a hot company's stock may disappear if the stock price drops.

- Be prepared to walk away. Being prepared to lose also prepares you to walk away. It helps you keep your integrity because you won't be in a situation where your need seems so great you're willing to compromise what you shouldn't. If you know you can walk away, it's easier to say no.

- Learn to be content. You can lose or walk away because you're content in any situation. You don't confuse your desires with your needs, a trap that causes you to overreach your capabilities and resources. I read an article about people who take on too much debt, the repayment of which drove them from their homes and cost them the possessions they acquired because it was so high. Being content gives you the luxury of being able to make wise choices.

- Take time to do it right the first time so you're not tempted to take a short cut later. Short cuts under pressure turn into long lasting pain. Carpenters like to say, "Measure twice, cut once."
- Don't avoid opportunities to be accountable to others. Because "Iron sharpens iron, So one man sharpens another" (Proverbs 27:17), being accountable to someone else helps you work out the alignment of your words, thoughts, deeds, and values so you're the same on Monday as you are on Sunday.

Social disciplines are important for establishing continuity in a group, whether it's the family, community, or nation, and help ensure that everyone is treated in a consistent way. Among those who've committed to follow the way of Christ, social disciplines can be an effective way of showing the humility others will see as love for each other, because "By this all men will know that you are My [Christ's] disciples, if you have love for one another" (John 13:35).

- Group traditions and rituals can be the glue that holds a group together. The airports are jammed at Thanksgiving and Christmas and the phone lines reach capacity on Mothers Day because of that glue. Don't neglect those traditions and rituals in your life and respect the traditions and rituals of others. They can often be a way to connect people back to God. For example, ancient Christians used the celebrations of other cultures to create analogies to the Gospel, drawing from sources like the ancient Roman custom of decorating trees and a pagan custom of burning a log that symbolized the turning of the year to create the Christmas tree and Yule log.
- Etiquette is an important social discipline, demonstrating concern for the feelings of others and acting like a lubricant to make personal interactions easier. There are many good books on etiquette and you can also look up information about etiquette on the Internet.

- "Proprieties" is a good word for the kinds of social disciplines that encourage restraint and modesty. For example, the way you act, speak, and dress gives clues about your character and capacity. In one of my favorite movies, *The Quiet Man*, the character played by John Wayne begins a formal courtship of the character played by Maureen O'Hara. As they start, their chaperone warns, "No patty-fingers, if you please. The proprieties at all times." As a way of drawing conclusions about people, this may not the most accurate way to get at who they are, but observing proprieties is an effective way of communicating that you care about the impression you make on others.

6

BECOME *GOD'S BLESSING* TO OTHERS
BY BECOMING A SERVANT

It's not enough to know what to do about your friendship with God because that knowledge creates a burden to take action. And knowledge turned into action is love. In fact, Paul's monumental description of love to his Corinthian readers in chapter 13 of his first letter contains all the elements for completely understanding it. And Jesus' example not only defines love, it also reveals it as a central component to God's character. All you've read to this point is part of a process bringing you to a point where you know how to love. But knowing what love is doesn't completely explain how it becomes evidence faith has turned into knowledge and knowledge into action.

The degree to which others see love in you is the degree to which they see you as a servant. Like the wind, they can't see love, but like the wind's effects, they can see servanthood. Jesus assured His followers, "By this all men will know that you are My disciples, if you have love for one another" (James 13:34, 35). That's the quality that sets you apart and servanthood is the visible evidence of that quality. In fact, it's the only way your life will have an impact on others.

When you make God's priorities your priorities, you begin seeing from God's perspective, that is, aligning your character so you reflect more of His character and knowing what He would do. Now it's time to do something about it. That's because what you're called to do isn't something like a career or any of the activities making up your day. You're called to love. And action you take based on your new priorities reveals that love.

Action based on love, that is, acting on the burden that comes from making God's priorities your priorities, is what servants do. I can quickly rattle off the names of history's great leaders, but I'd have to work a lot harder to think of the names of history's great servants. But that's the point. There's no hall of fame in this world for servants, only halls to clean. Even the ones I know about in stories tend to get short shrift.

Rudyard Kipling's Gunga Din, a fictional water carrier in India serving a British army regiment in the nineteenth century, had to die saving the life of one of the British soldiers before being recognized for his qualities. And think about the controversial Uncle Tom. When you read Harriet Beecher Stowe's novel, *Uncle Tom's Cabin*, you find that Uncle Tom is a slave of godly character who transformed his role into one of significance. But today, calling someone Uncle Tom is using the name as a derogatory epithet. Even fictional servants don't get a break from this world.

So why put up with that ignominy? Because it's part of the job description. Being a servant is never about getting something for yourself but about ensuring what's best for others. That mindset comes because God's priorities have replaced your priorities, giving you a duty to meet God's needs.

How can the God Who created the universe have needs? In Jesus' description of the final judgment, He commends some, saying, "I was hungry, and you gave Me something to eat; I was thirsty, and you gave Me something to drink; I was a stranger, and you invited Me in; naked, and you clothed Me; I was sick, and you visited Me; I was in prison, and you came to Me" (Matthew 25:35,36). The "I" to whom Jesus was referring was Himself, identifying Himself with the world's greatest needs. And God's needs are the needs of the world for compassion, decency, and holy living. So meeting those needs is how you go about your Master's business.

Those examples highlight the point of servants' existence: they serve because it's who they are, what they know, and what they do. In other words, they fix their identities on their subordinate roles, which become the lens through which others see them. And when God identifies Himself with the needs others experience in this world, servants take it upon themselves to meet those needs.

So others see servants through the prism of those roles, that is, they have a mental picture of what servants do and expect those who are identified as servants to act that way. That's why Jesus was so disruptive. He called Himself a king but acted like a servant. In other words, He changed the expected role of one who leads by becoming one who serves.

Just how does love become visible as servanthood? Paul gave his Philippian readers an anatomy of love as servanthood in the second chapter of his letter to them. Trying to explain why he wanted his readers to regard each other in love, he pointed them to Jesus as their example, describing how Jesus left His high station in heaven for death on a cross (Philippians 2:5-9). Paul didn't dwell much on Jesus' intentions or feelings but on Jesus' actions as evidence of His intent.

The acronym SERVE helps explain how that attitude shows up as action. It's a set of characteristics that are the results of the processes explained in this book. They are:

- Subordinate your priorities
- Empty your pride
- Redirect your potential
- Vacate your position
- Exalt Him who purchased you

In other words, God designs everything you experience to bring you to this point.

Subordinate your priorities. Subordinating your priorities begins your experience as a servant after you begin seeing from God's perspective. And Paul wants his readers to make the same transition, directing them to "Have this attitude in yourselves which was also in Christ Jesus" (Philippians 2:5). From the moment you become God's friend, everything has been a lesson in setting your priorities aside and taking up God's priorities.

Empty your pride. Pride is your regard for your own capabilities and can be a powerful driving force. The ancient Greeks called it *hubris*, an attitude of overreaching we see in the serpent's challenge to Eve that eating the fruit would make her like God. Well, Jesus wasn't just like God, He was God. But "although He existed in the form of God, did not regard equality with God a thing to be grasped, but emptied Himself" (Philippians 2:6-7a). So the only reaching out and grasping you do is in dependency on God Himself because He brings you to a realization nothing else you grab is secure.

Redirect your potential. When you have a regard for your capabilities, you develop a vision of where those capabilities can take you. That vision is your potential. It's the old saw, "You can do anything if you put your mind to it." And you may be familiar with other motivational sayings meant to inspire people to keep striving for the brass ring. But for Jesus, it meant "taking the form of a bond-servant, and being made in the likeness of men" (Philippians 2:7b). After emptying your pride, you also give up regard for your own capabilities to do things and depend on God's capabilities.

Vacate your position. You may already be at the point you want to be or you may still be striving for what you think is owed you. For Jesus, however, it meant giving up the sovereign kingship due Him because "Being found in appearance as a man, He humbled Himself by becoming obedient to the point of death, even death on a cross" (Philippians 2:8). Jesus' example points you away from achieving your goals and to letting God achieve His goals through you.

Exalt Him who purchased you. Jesus' actions exalted God, so "For this reason also, God highly exalted Him, and bestowed on Him the name which is above every name" (Philippians 2:9). His actions exalted God because they directed attention to God. Likewise, your actions can do the same.

Remember the lessons of BOASTS earlier in this book? Boasting about how God turned you into the friend He wants you to be is how you can exalt Him because you're directing attention to Him.

Becoming a servant puts you on the path toward transforming the world. How can that be? Aren't servants the powerless ones whom the world easily and instinctively knocks down? Aren't they the ones who should know their place, rarely seen and never heard? Aren't they the ones who use the back door so distinguished guests don't see them? Yes, yes, and yes.

And that's why God can use you to transform that same world. Not respected by this world, your low standing forces you to look toward Jesus Christ for sustenance and point others toward Him for credit. Because you go through experiences that make you the friend God wants you to be and teach you what to do about it through turning God's priorities into your priorities, you have nowhere else to which you can point others.

What a relief. Becoming a servant frees you from the stress of climbing the pyramid because it turns the pyramid upside down. While there's little room at the top, there's plenty of room at the bottom. That change in the direction you're climbing can change the world.

So although servants take different forms, each one a lesson on an aspect of obedience, the predominant image is that of the slave because that was who served in the ancient world. Slaves did the menial work and had no rights. They were utterly disposable, and in some ancient cultures, their masters could arbitrarily kill them.

In fact, some argue that William Wilberforce's great achievement was not so much convincing Great Britain to end slavery (although that was a truly significant accomplishment) but to make commonplace the idea that slavery was wrong. Up to that point, slavery was an accepted institution, and entire societies took it as a matter-of-fact part of the scenery, even giving highly competent slaves great responsibility. But even those slaves had no rights or assets and were subject to their masters' whims.

As a prospective servant, then, place yourself in first century culture to understand the degree of humility that comes with job. There are no rights, no compensation, and no rest. You serve the master's wishes and have no claim to your own desires. That's consistent with Jesus Christ's example. His entire life on earth, from His adolescent reminder to His parents He was about His Father's business to His prayer in Gethsemane, "not as I will, but as You will" (Matthew 26:39), was marked by such a servant's attitude. And He punctuated it with gestures like washing the disciples' feet.

When love takes the form of servanthood, it's clear love isn't a feeling of friendship, good intent, or romance. You may not like someone, but you're still called to love him or her. And that means serving that person. Nor is servanthood a visible mark like a tattoo, logo, or bumper sticker. It's not something you tell the world to get credit as if it were a line on your resume.

But being a servant doesn't mean you shouldn't speak out. God's needs for this world include justice and mercy, and just as servants need to look after their masters' best interests, you have the opportunity to look out for God's best interests by pursuing His desire for the world. And sometimes it means confronting others with truth.

In fact, becoming a servant can actually make you bold because "perfect love casts out fear" (I John 4:18). You may know examples of courage, from the mother risking her own life to save her children to soldiers sacrificing their lives to save their comrades. That's because when you have come to love God deeply, you're willing to risk greatly to be God's blessing to others.

I recall spending an evening at a dinner banquet chatting with a soft-spoken gentleman sitting next to me. At the end of the dinner, the host stood up, made a short speech, and then said,

"Would the Medal of Honor recipients please stand up to be recognized." This gentleman stood up. I had been in the presence of one of the United States' greatest heroes who loved the lives of his comrades so much more than his own that he braved bullets and rockets to go to their rescue.

The degree of love that causes courageous acts epitomizes the servant's heart. It's a degree of love that not only moves people to individual feats of physical courage like war heroes, it moves people to feats of moral courage. The media is full of examples of individuals and groups that stand up for various causes, but the moral courage generated by a servant's love involves pointing others to Jesus Christ and inviting them to take up their unfinished business.

But notable feats aren't the only way servants display courage. They display it by taking up their responsibilities every day even when it doesn't seem to be worthwhile or make sense. Rather than walking out on marriages, they stay and work every day to make the relationships work. And instead of giving up on life, they get up every morning, go to work, and come home to attend to their families. They give up their own desires and goals to attend their children's ball games, mow their elderly parents' lawns, and support their communities and churches.

They do these mundane things because they understand their unfinished business is a way of living that permeates every nook and cranny of life. And others watch. Having heard the talk about taking up their unfinished business, they want to see the evidence of it in servants' lives. So it's the small displays of servanthood everyday that prove servants not only know what to do about their friendship with God, it shows they've turned that knowledge into action.

7

BECOMING A SERVANT IS AN UPWARD PATH

There's a path to becoming a servant at home, at work, at school, and in your community. Recall that God presented you with unfinished business when He made you His friend, and He refined that friendship by allowing circumstances into your life. That character development makes God's perspective clear and turns His priorities into your priorities when you increase in the four dimensions of your life. And knowledge of that perspective becomes action because it compels you to do something about it.

But becoming a servant doesn't just happen. Turning faith into knowledge and knowledge into action is a program of deliberate change, the dynamics behind pursuing your unfinished business. To remember this process, think of the acronym UPWARD, which lists the components of your growth, a systematic way to turn the faith that made you God's friend into knowledge of His perspective and finally into a servant's actions that makes you His blessing to others. UPWARD is:

- Understand the situation
- Purpose in your heart
- Wait on God
- Act decisively
- Reflect deeply
- Devote yourself completely

A systematic way to think about your development makes you more effective in pursuing your unfinished business because you can be methodical and deliberate about it. What a relief. But what a challenge also because it means anyone of us can do it. So we don't have excuses. And without a systematic understanding of your development, it's hard to appreciate the importance of continually developing and growing. Because you have a free will, it's tempting to choose not to keep moving upward because it takes less effort. But if you're not moving upward, you're sliding back down.

When my children were still in high school, I asked them what they thought the toughest part of college would be. They tossed out ideas like harder subjects and more costs, but I told them it would be freedom. Without a conscious commitment to a way of living, young people experiencing the freedoms of college for the first time where no one tells them when to get up in the morning or pushes them in the numerous areas where parents used to push can find it easy to abuse their new situations.

You too have great personal freedom, a condition that exposes you to things that can distract you from pursuing your unfinished business. Taking on the discipline of a systematic approach to growth will help you stay on track.

That's because it forces you to look deep into yourself and confront those areas you have to change. You won't like it at times, but if you're honest with yourself, you'll make steady and sometimes spectacular progress. It can even give you cause for optimism because you have something to look forward to as well as something purposeful to work at.

So the UPWARD process is really a virtuous circle. That is, working through all the steps of UPWARD positions you for another cycle of growth because you uncover more areas in which you can develop. This ongoing cycle of improvement shows up in all four dimensions of your life and is visible to those around you.

UPWARD gives you a way to turn faith into knowledge and knowledge into action, the actual mechanism of perfecting that completes you in all four dimensions. That's because rather than focusing on externals, Jesus dealt with the heart, saying your thoughts have the same impact as your actions.

And at even deeper levels than your thoughts, UPWARD refines your desires in all four dimensions, changing them from desires that are self-oriented to desires for what God

116

wants. This is what "happily ever after" can be for you —
discovering your unfinished business and embarking on a
journey of perpetual growth to become God's blessing for others.

Understand the situation

When I was starting a military career as a young officer,
one of the training methodologies involved reviewing knotty
scenarios that required a decision. The instructors invariably
challenged the new officers with the question, "What now,
lieutenant?" And the professors of business courses I studied
gave their students case studies to dissect, reminding the students
there were no right or wrong answers to those situations, only
well-analyzed recommendations.

In both experiences, the military instructors and business
professors insisted on first defining the problem presented. This
was easier said than done, the business students often arguing
among themselves issues like whether a money-losing
company's problem was a poor marketing strategy or inefficient
production processes. Like those students preparing their case
studies, a critical step in your UPWARD development is to
understand the situation you're in.

You face the challenge of sifting through information
that may not be relevant as well as recognizing the influence of
your assumptions on your thinking. A number of German
Christians recognized the danger behind the message of a rising
politician in the 1930s. After Hitler became Chancellor of
Germany, he began consolidating his power and included among
his actions forcing the organized Christian churches to support
Nazism.

But it was easy to go along. In the 1930s, the devastation
of World War I and the Great Depression still vivid experiences,
the sense of order and purpose the new leader provided was
restoring the confidence of the nation, and there was pressure to
conform.

But some Christians understood that Nazism and their faith were incompatible and resisted. They saw through what Hitler was promising because they looked through the lens of their unfinished business. They understood the unpleasantness of their nation's circumstances wasn't reason enough to go along. In other words, they had a clear understanding of the situation.

Your commitment to pursuing your unfinished business is the framework for understanding your situation because it helps you see a pattern in your circumstances. Just like sneezing, a runny nose, and a headache are symptoms of a cold, your circumstances can be the symptoms of what got you to your current situation and indicators of your possible next steps.

Understanding your situation, therefore, means seeing beyond your circumstances no matter how pressing or pleasurable. Students understand that concept well. Some may not apply it as well as others, but all students get it. In the middle of the term when class projects are coming due and big tests are coming up, students know not to be distracted by the pressures of deadlines that are the circumstances pressing down on them. It would be too easy to give up and go home to something easier.

Instead, they persevere because they look past their present circumstances to their real goal — graduation and career success. They understand the greater good behind the current pressures and act in ways that will get them closer to that greater good. They keep up with their homework, join study groups, and get research help as they need it.

But understanding your situation isn't the same as finding the answer. It's tempting to jump to what you think is the answer, but be aware the pressure of your immediate circumstances and unexamined assumptions can lead to the wrong conclusions. Have you heard the joke about the researchers and the spider?

Several researchers put a spider on a table and commanded, "Walk!" The spider scurried quickly across. A researcher put the spider on a piece of flypaper and commanded,

"Walk!" The spider sat in one spot, stuck. The researchers concluded, "Spiders go deaf when placed on flypaper." Without taking the time to understand your situation, you can make the wrong connections between cause and effect like those hapless researchers.

Don't think that light-hearted example means jumping to conclusions isn't a big deal. When the bubonic plague and other related diseases swept Europe in the fourteenth century, killing millions in the Black Death, the medieval Europeans attributed the disaster to a number of causes: punishment by God for sins, poisoning by the Jews, and the inopportune appearance of a comet.

In fact, the plague came from germs and was helped along by the poor hygienic practices of the age. But those misconceptions and lack of knowledge kept victims from being properly treated and led to large economic upheavals because of massive depopulation. It also undermined confidence in the institutional church because the leaders couldn't satisfactorily explain why the Black Death was happening.

Although understanding your situation isn't the same as finding a solution, it does mean you can narrow down the possible causes and solutions. When I was still in college and dating the woman who would later become my wife, I was in my dorm room gluing a photograph of her to a wood plaque as part of decoupage project. I had just learned the basics of the craft. While I was trimming and gluing the photograph, I was telling a friend that I wasn't sure how I could tell how seriously I felt about this woman. He laughed and said, "You're sitting there building a monument to her and you don't know how you feel about her?" That narrowed things down for me — that's when I realized I was in love with her.

Put God's perspective into action. When you make God's priorities your priorities, you're able to see past your present circumstances to the higher purpose behind those priorities. Paul confidently assured Timothy that "the Lord will give you understanding in everything" (II Timothy 2:7) because while Timothy had a finite perspective, Paul understood God's infinite perspective. You won't see His entire plan until you see Him face to face, but you'll see enough of His plan to understand your situation.

Recall what others have done. When you think about what others have gone through, you'll realize you're not alone, that others have experienced the same thing in the past and that others are experiencing the same thing now. This is important because it's easier to give up if you think you're by yourself.

Purpose in your heart

Purposing in your heart commits you to aligning yourself with God's general will for your life. This is the foundation of true accountability — you're trusted with ways to live and are called to exercise the discipline needed to follow through on your decision.

When Paul wrote to the church members in Corinth about giving money for church work, he stressed to his readers the importance of giving voluntarily without feeling compelled, concluding, "Each one must do just as he has purposed in his heart" (II Corinthians 9:7). All the words used in the ancient manuscripts that translate into the verb form of "purpose" refer to some form of making a proposal to oneself, a statement of intention that sets the stage for future action.

It's like preparing to drive across the country. You may not know the route yet, but you already know you can do some things to prepare. Travel routes and destinations may be different for everyone, but everyone does similar things to prepare for a long drive. You check the oil like everyone else, changing it if needed. You check the tires like everyone else, filling them with air if a bit low. You even prepare for emergencies like everyone else, making sure you pack a first aid kit.

Purposing in your heart to follow God's general will is like preparing for that trip. You may not know what specific thing you should be doing yet, so you focus on following God's general will. For example, David asked for God's attention in one of the Psalms, confident that God would hold him innocent because among other claims to innocence against various slanders and affirming, "I have purposed that my mouth will not transgress" (Psalm 17:3).

So purposing in your heart is a commitment to narrowing your options. Just as you narrow your options when getting ready to drive across the country (for example, you would probably leave the snow chains at home for a summer trip), purposing in your heart commits you to narrowing your options in responding to your circumstances.

For example, you know from the Ten Commandments that God has certain expectations for relating to Him and your fellow humans. Those expectations give you a framework for making sound choices because committing to them means turning away from options that keep you from living according to those expectations.

Relying on that framework gives substance to your character, a solid thing that creates an impression the way an object displaces water. The more there is to the object, the more water it displaces. It's no accident the term for the impression you make is called *gravitas*, a Latin word from which we get "gravity."

Just as gravity is stronger on those planets that have a larger presence in space (a 150 pound person on earth would weigh over 350 pounds on Jupiter), the dignity and seriousness others see in you is greater because the *gravitas* created by your commitment to God's general will is the result of His greater presence in you.

And it's one of several qualities you display after you've stayed focused on God's general will for a time. Qualities like prudence, dignity, courage, faith, and love are nothing more than the evidence of godly knowledge made real.

Purposing in your heart doesn't mean following a legalistic set of codes. While your knowledge of God's general will is enough to apply to specific life situations, it doesn't have to be rigid and unbending because God wants you to understand the intent behind the words, the gist of Jesus' preaching during the three years He walked around Palestine.

While Jesus knew that Jewish law mandated death for an adulterous woman, for example, He wanted to teach the people that a pure heart was what mattered. Those who brought the woman before Him thought they had put Jesus in a bind. If Jesus agreed with the penalty, He would be supporting the current understanding of Jewish law He claimed to fulfill and possibly creating a conflict with the Roman occupation forces that reserved capital punishment for themselves. But if He didn't, He could be accused of subverting the Law and disobeying God.

So Jesus found a third way. Saying, "He who is without sin among you, let him be the first to throw a stone at her" (John 8:7), He challenged the accusers to prove their motives were pure and then showed that God was a God of second chances when He forgave the woman. But second chances also call for a change in life direction, as Jesus reminded the woman when He told her, "From now on sin no more" (John 8:11).

That means following God's general will isn't based on rewards and punishments either — it's based on a relationship. It's part of how you increase in favor. Remember that favoring someone can mean looking like that person. When you start to display the virtues commended in the Bible, you begin to resemble God because those virtues are an extension of His character. Rewards and punishments may affect what you do, but a relationship affects who you are.

Paradoxically, purposing in your heart to follow God's general will narrows your focus and widens your vision. It narrows your focus from the transient nature of this world and its cornucopia of temptations to the eternal work of God. When Jesus contrasted the wide and narrow gates, He had that in mind.

And it widens your vision by helping you make connections between what you may have overlooked and what God wants for this world. Because Isaac Newton committed to believing God created the universe, he believed God would have made it orderly, an assumption that helped him develop his great theories of gravity and mechanics.

Martin Luther and William Tyndale among others, believing God wanted to speak directly to everyone, stopped taking the privileged position of the clergy for granted and translated the Bible, originally available only in Latin, into their native tongues. And David Wilkerson stopped overlooking the distasteful world of teenage gangs and founded Teen Challenge.

Because you can readily apply God's general will to specific life situations, you can sometimes determine your responses in advance. Because others have experienced similar situations, mentors and friends with whom you share your thoughts and intentions can help you prepare. They help you clarify God's general will and, by discussing your understanding, help you rehearse your responses.

Rehearsal is important because it makes you confident you can respond to particular situations and gives you resilience in the face of unexpected things. Someone who purposes in his or her heart to join a mission trip to help victims of a natural disaster knows it can't be scheduled far ahead of time — natural disasters tend not to make appointments. But rehearsing the response, that is, finding out what's required for such a trip, ensures doing things like updating the passport, setting money aside in a trip fund, and getting some work clothes.

That's important — knowing and following God's specific will, as you'll read later, gives you a deep impact on the world, but following His general will gives you a broad impact, allowing you to affect people in the common areas of life. For example, a married couple I know has an impact in the common area of marriage, and I've heard younger people say, "I want to have a marriage like theirs."

Wait on God

Purposing in your heart to follow God's general will prepares you to seek God's specific will, that is, what He would have you do because you're the exact person He's chosen for the task. But there's a twist. Normally, when you want something specific or you want to get a task done, you get right to it and become agitated at the lack of progress. You don't want to sit around because you can't get wasted time back.

I watch a show with my wife that follows a company as it buys old houses and buildings, renovates them, and sells them at a profit. Invariably, it shows them confronting contractors and pushing the project impatiently because they're on short timelines.

It's fun to watch and illustrates a fundamental truth about our natures — we don't want to be idle when something needs to get done. But waiting on God confronts that desire to get things done because it takes the initiative out of your hands and gives it to God.

Purposing in your heart makes it possible to wait on God. Remember when you commit yourself to God's general will, you find it narrows your focus and widens your vision. You can remove distractions so you can concentrate on important things, and you begin to look at life from an eternal perspective, removing the pressure of having to respond according to the transient nature of this world.

You no longer feel like you have to seize the day because it gives you something greater to seize, a deeper relationship with God. This prepares you to wait on God because you can look beyond the expediencies of the moment.

Where purposing in your heart is like preparing for a long drive, waiting on God is like making that drive. Each journey is different for everyone. And each journey takes some time to complete. As good as any of us might be at reading the road map and even at finding short cuts, that journey must take time, something we don't necessarily appreciate. We know we don't like the time it takes to get to our destinations because we understand the child's question, "Are we there yet?"

Waiting on God to know His specific will involves preparation that is out of your hands. It's a shaping that takes place to make you fit the requirements of the task. If you've ever tried finding a job or hiring someone for a job, you understand the importance of fit. But where employers look for people who already fit their requirements, God takes the time and effort to shape you so you fit His needs.

So just because God wants you for a particular task doesn't mean you're ready to start doing it. God chose Samson to be a judge, one of a series of great men whom God selected to protect Israel against her enemies. Samson possessed astounding strength but lost it all because he wasn't prepared for the tests of character that come from such great responsibility.

That means a lot happens while you wait on God. John Newton waited on God to discover His specific will by continuing his sailing work while pursuing his disciplines. A slaver by trade in the late eighteenth century, he converted to Christianity but continued sailing while studying Latin and the Bible. But after a time, he realized that part of God's specific will for him was to leave the slave trade, so he took a government position on shore and continued his studies.

After several years, he began a series of moves that culminated in his position as a full-time pastor of a church and author of a number of hymns, his first being the famous "Amazing Grace." So even though Newton was in another job for a number of years, he was experiencing the preparation and change that fitted him to be a pastor. People who wait on God are marked by that prioritization of their efforts.

Therefore, waiting on God is neither passivity nor busy work. It's purposeful effort God uses to shape you into the right fit for His specific will. It includes returning to His general will through the disciplines and mentorship from others who have traveled that path. Newton had the examples of George Whitefield and John Wesley and befriended William Cowper, a great English poet. Eventually, Newton became William Wilberforce's mentor as that young politician sought God's specific will, a chain of mentorship that eventually ended slavery in the British Empire.

Usually, when you want to perform a certain task, you develop skills specific to that task. When you want a certain job, you tout your ability to do that job. God takes that approach away from you. Paul the Apostle thought he could do a better job if God would take away an unidentified thorn in the flesh, but God responded, "My grace is sufficient for you, for power is perfected in weakness" (II Corinthians 12:9).

So it turns out your fit for God's specific will revolves around your lack of ability to pull it off yourself. Gideon, the inspiration for modern Israel's special operations forces, had to make do with 300 men against an army of thousands because God whittled his group of volunteers down from 32,000, using seemingly arbitrary selection criteria like how they drank water from a stream.

Waiting on God to find out His specific will is when you should be telling yourself truth. That is, you should dwell on objective truth instead of how you feel at that moment. It reminds you of that to which you're committed and takes you beyond transient feelings because waiting can otherwise be a frustrating time.

Continuing your spiritual disciplines is how you tell yourself truth. They're activities like prayer, worship, Bible study, meditation, fellowship, service, tithing, and evangelism. I know I have to admit that my exercise of the disciplines is less than best, but that's all the more reason to stay focused, not a reason to get discouraged or an excuse to do even less.

That's because exercising spiritual disciplines calls you to sacrifice conflicting activities. Daily living out Paul's exhortation to "lay aside every encumbrance, and the sin which so easily entangles us, and ... run with endurance the race that is set before us" (Hebrews 12:1) will help you turn your knowledge of God's priorities into action.

Act decisively

Acting decisively is the area where you commit to what you understand is God's specific will for you. You're like the apostle Peter in the story, *Quo Vadis*, who, fleeing persecution in Rome, abruptly turned around and went back to death from the persecutors. He explained to his friends that he had just seen a vision of Jesus asking him, "Quo vadis, Peter?" Which way, Peter? And Peter, who had denied Jesus in the courtyard, knew his place was in Rome with the other persecuted Christians. Acting decisively is your "quo vadis" moment — no more questions about God's general will and waiting to discover God's specific will for you.

You can act decisively because you not only know it's the right decision, you know you have the endurance to see it through. Your practices strengthen your mind and spirit so you can carry out another task in the unfinished business God has presented to you. Because you're not approaching it as if you could do it yourself, you have the confidence that God has equipped you for it. Whether they're words, thoughts, or deeds, your actions reflect the degree to which your knowledge and will are integrated with what God expects.

Acting decisively isn't a time for hesitation and half-measures. It's the difference between bacon and eggs — the pig is committed, the chicken isn't. I was told by a businessman that entrepreneurs can impress potential investors by showing that they've committed everything to their venture. If they can show, for example, that they took out a second mortgage to fund the fledgling business, potential investors are more likely to provide additional money.

Acting decisively is another phrase for being a martyr. No, I'm not telling you to go face lethal persecution. But I am suggesting that your commitment allows you to enact Paul's charge to "present your bodies a living and holy sacrifice" (Romans 12:1). Acting decisively reflects your level of commitment characterized by an attitude of no turning back.

Historical examples of that kind of decisiveness include Alexander the Great. He burned his ships after landing in Persia to demonstrate the level of commitment to his invasion that he expected from himself and his soldiers. And Julius Caesar understood that when he crossed the Rubicon River with his legions, he was effectively starting a civil war in Rome. If those leaders were willing to commit all for kingdoms that would pass away, how much more those of us who claim to serve the Creator of the universe?

You can act decisively because of the intense preparation God has provided you. It's a deliberate approach to life, the same approach the Founding Fathers took when they pledged their lives and sacred honor to break with Great Britain. The Declaration of Independence wasn't an impulsive act but the culmination of centuries of philosophical thought about government and where citizens should have their allegiance.

The disciples made that commitment when Jesus said, "Follow me." Matthew left a lucrative occupation as tax collector, and Peter and James left the familiar work of fishing to which they had been raised. Paul incurred the wrath of his Pharisaical colleagues when he embraced the religion he once persecuted. You probably won't have to take drastic action like they did, but you should plan to honor your commitment.

Acting decisively takes different forms depending on the situation. Sometimes it can be incremental, that is, small actions that have a profound effect. Jesus commended the widow who could only donate a pittance over those who gave much money. She gave all, but the rich gave out of their plenty. It's these small actions based on great commitment, He preached, upon which the kingdom of Heaven is based because they can have great impact.

There's no guarantee you won't make mistakes. On the contrary, many have told me they don't think they're fully committed if they aren't making some mistakes — as much as you want to know that you're acting on God's specific will, you're human and should expect a margin of error. However, that margin can be smaller if you've been prepared for your task. Peter made a mistake of avoiding Gentile Christians so he could stay in the favor of those Jewish Christians who still had a legalistic outlook, and Paul challenged him on it. But the cause of Christ still moved forward.

Acting decisively is evidence the burden of friendship with God and making His priorities your own has overflowed into action. Pentecost turned frightened disciples into fearless preachers when the Holy Spirit filled them. These were men who hid and even denied knowing Jesus at the time of Jesus' crucifixion, but at Pentecost, they astounded Jerusalem and set into motion the expansion of Christianity. That's because they were harnessed to a purpose, meek people who accomplished astounding things.

Meekness is often confused with weakness. That's because it's actually a commitment to pursue a higher goal, requiring you to back away from pursuing material goals. Jesus' prediction that the meek shall inherit the earth is actually an ironic statement pointing out that meek people are actually the aggressors.

When you think of taking over the world, you think of conquerors like Genghis Khan, Alexander the Great, and Napoleon. They may have cast giant shadows for a time, but their empires receded and in dying, they inherited nothing but earth.

This is the point then where you "prove yourselves doers of the word, and not merely hearers who delude themselves" (James 1:22). If you stay at the level of understanding your situation, purposing in your heart to follow God's general will, and waiting on God for His specific will, you're a spectator. If you want to be a player, you have to get in the game.

Acting decisively gets you off the bench and onto the field. The burden you feel for getting in the game is called a sense of urgency, the same sense of urgency communicated by Paul that "now is the day of salvation" (II Corinthians 6:2) when he encouraged his Corinthian readers to show their faith well. It lets you put feet on God's specific will for you and makes you God's blessing to others.

Reflect deeply

Up to now, the components of UPWARD you've been following to turn faith into knowledge and knowledge into action are similar to many formulas for personal growth. But reflecting deeply on what you've experienced takes you beyond what most people consider personal development. Development models are oriented to techniques; that is, when you review the outcomes of your experience, you're interested in understanding if you fell short of what you expected and what you should do to make up the difference.

For example, this step might be called "Review analytically" in other models of development because you would review the outcomes of the actions you took, comparing the results with what you wanted to achieve and developing ways to close the gaps in areas you identified as falling short.

Reflecting deeply takes you in a different direction, causing you to use the outcomes of your actions to understand the degree to which God's priorities have become your priorities in the four dimensions of your life. It shows you where you must rearrange your world view, an act that goes deeper than simply fixing where you fall short. It involves revising your assumptions, changing the fundamental beliefs you treat as facts in the absence because you don't have perfect knowledge. In other words, it takes you back to the beginning to reexamine the basics of your faith, so you can turn that in which you hope into outward acts of love.

Socrates asserted the unexamined life wasn't worth living, so this is your opportunity to clear out dead attitudes and assumptions that weigh you down. But many are too busy to give it much thought, acknowledging that reflection is important but not seriously engaging in it. In a way, this is understandable because reflection is like doing your homework.

But it's also too bad because homework is what helps the lessons sink in. If you sit in class and listen to the teacher, you absorb part of the lesson, but if you do the assigned homework, you absorb much more. Homework shows you how to apply the teaching points so you can turn the material into actual results.

Reflecting deeply is closely related to meekness because it involves recasting your spirit. If meekness, as some scholars would tell you, evokes the image of a powerful horse harnessed for productive use, then reflecting deeply is like the process by which that horse is transformed from an independent animal to one that made it productive. Horse training techniques include keeping the horse focused and responsive to the trainer and being consistent in treating the horse, neither being easy with rewards nor harsh with punishment. Reflecting deeply takes you down the path of sharpening your focus on God.

If you review the outcomes of business decisions, you would ask questions like these:

- What was the intended outcome? You would want to remember what you wanted to achieve.
- What was the actual outcome? You would want to clearly know what really happened as a result of your actions.
- Why did things turn out the way they did? You would determine why the outcome came out the way it did so you could understand the cause.
- What can I do to improve the actual outcome? You would list things you could do better next time.

But reflecting deeply takes a different tack. Because you want be more productive in God's terms, you can't stop at improving what you do. Those are external, and God is interested in changing what's inside.

When He claims, "I, the Lord, search the heart, I test the mind" (Jeremiah 17:10), He's saying He intends to dive deep and bring you with Him because He wants to refine who you are as His friend and keep you on track with where you're going so you can become even more aligned to His priorities. This helps you pursue your unfinished business more effectively because it helps you become even more of a blessing to others.

You know you're diving deep when you begin to attach accountability to more and more of your decisions. Being accountable for your choices means you can acknowledge you're not a victim of forces beyond your control because you trust that God is ultimately in control. Corrie Ten Boom, author of *The Hiding Place*, talked about her experiences in the Nazi concentration camps during World War Two and told a story about forgiving one of her former captors who came to her asking for forgiveness. She was able to forgive because God had replaced her bitterness with love.

While reflecting deeply includes intellectual effort, it's not intellectualizing. That is, it's not a way to abstract the issue so you can avoid personal accountability for your choices. Intellectualizing helps you avoid personal accountability because you stay detached, looking at the outcomes of your actions as if they were collectibles, objects to be examined and then put back on the shelf. You can tell when you're intellectualizing because you don't personally identify with what you're examining and you don't contemplate the possibility of change.

You develop godly perception when you dive deep because you see more clearly what your character is really like. Reflecting deeply also has a double meaning — the act of examining yourself is like a mirror reflecting back a true image. And it also means holding up that mirror continually.

Remember, the same admonishment to be doers and not hearers likens the difference to "a man who looks at his natural face in a mirror; for once he has looked at himself and gone away, he has immediately forgotten what kind of person he was" (James 1:23-24). That willingness to dive deep makes you transparent as well because you're also willing to be accountable to others, who can help you because they can see you from the outside.

And there's even a third meaning. Reflecting deeply helps you reflect brightly because God uses the occasion to polish specific parts of your character so you reflect His character more brightly. That's because you integrate the lessons of your experiences into your thinking so they become patterns you can recognize in the future.

You also shape your assumptions so they form a sturdier foundation for future choices. This kind of reflection shapes you from the inside out because you tend to become like that which you think about the most, echoing that Biblical idea that "as he thinks within himself, so he is" (Proverbs 23:7).

This is the time to pry open those hidden places where your assumptions form your world view. Those hidden places are where you're really yourself because no one can see in, reminding you of the popular phrase that character is who you are when no one's looking. It's easy to think you've aligned yourself with God, but you're human and always have more changes to make.

For example, choices made in the privacy of our homes can accurately reflect our priorities. It's no surprise the increasingly available private entertainment options like rental videos you can watch at home, pay-per-view television, and the Internet are matched by rising revenues for the pornography and gambling industries. These forms of entertainment, once kept in check by the public venues where people had to go, have exploded in popularity because of their availability in the privacy of people's homes. But we're really not alone — our company is God as well as the person we see in the mirror every day.

One way to search those hidden places is to set time aside for such reflection. For example, you might go on a personal retreat. It doesn't have to be a specific location like an actual retreat center but can be as simple as going behind a closed door in your home for a while. But remember the purpose of a retreat is to retreat, not relax. It's called a retreat because you're withdrawing for a reason.

Here are some ways you can make that time of reflection profitable:

- Become familiar with the lives of people you admire, and speculate on how they might have acted in your circumstances. Of course, your supreme example is Jesus Christ, and you probably have seen people sporting bracelets to remind them to always ask the question, "What would Jesus do?"

- Open the hidden places of your life to scrutiny. This isn't an easy task. Even in the privacy your own thoughts it's understandable if you're reluctant to own up to some of the things you're doing. This is where you review your understanding of God's general will because those principles form the standard against which you can measure yourself.

- Make yourself transparent by being accountable to someone else. The give and take between you and your accountability partner can give you perspectives from which you can examine yourself more thoroughly.

- Be prepared to change your assumptions. Because we're not omniscient, we hold certain beliefs that take the place of facts we don't have. Some assumptions aren't pleasant to admit when we say we believe one thing but act in contrary ways. Be prepared to let go.

Devote yourself completely

Where acting decisively reflects the *depth* of your commitment, devoting yourself completely reflects the *scope* of your commitment because it's your chance to thoroughly internalize what you've learned. Although it sounds like an exercise in practical application of knowledge, it's really the completion of a thorough realignment of your priorities. But devotion *to* what and *of* what?

You realign your priorities based on what you learned in the previous steps. Understanding your situation and how God's will applies to it gives you the basis for any changes you have to make. Those changes bring you closer to what God expects from you and show up as a servant's actions.

When you examine the hidden places in your life with God, He shows what you must change. Devoting yourself completely uses what you discovered during that reflection to make those changes. Jesus told two stories to teach His listeners the degree of devotion they needed. In one story, a man found a treasure in a field, and in another story, a man found a very valuable pearl. In both cases, they sold everything to buy the object of their desire, the field containing the treasure and the pearl itself (Matthew 13:44-46).

In both cases, the men knew they could get a greater return on their investments than the price they paid, so they invested everything. That means devoting yourself completely is another way of being an effective steward of what God has presented you.

Complete devotion is a radical idea and inspires the radical language in Paul's declaration, "I have been crucified with Christ" (Galatians 2:20), to illustrate the scope and seriousness of this idea. Crucifixion was a deliberate and decisive act used by the ancient Romans to punish specific types of crime and deter potential wrong-doers.

One class of wrong-doers consisted of those who revolted against the government. That great movie, *Spartacus*, chronicled the unsuccessful flight to freedom of an army of gladiators and other slaves who had rebelled against their Roman masters. In the end, after losing a battle against Rome's legions, the surviving slaves were crucified as punishment for their rebellion. And the pretext for killing Jesus was His preaching about the kingdom of God, the words of which were twisted to support charges of sedition against Him.

Crucifixion was a favored execution method against rebels because it put them in a position where they could be seen by the public as if the Empire was saying, "You want people to follow you? They can follow you while you carry your cross. You want to be on top? Now everyone can look up at you." It put the victim on display to demonstrate the Empire's power and what would happen to anyone else who overreached.

Paul had that image in mind when he chose crucifixion as the metaphor to describe the completeness of devotion that comes from your upward quest. He regarded complete devotion as an act not just of leaving behind old ways but also hoisting them up in full view of the world to show what God had done in his life.

I'm not interested in telling others about my shortcomings, and I'm sure not interested in revealing skeletons in my closet. But that's exactly what Paul had in mind when he vowed, "may it never be that I would boast, except in the cross of our Lord Jesus Christ, through which the world has been crucified to me, and I to the world" (Galatians 6:14).

Devoting yourself completely means you have to die in order to live. That phrase isn't so strange if you think about it in everyday terms. When students have a test, they sacrifice some leisure time to study. At least that's what parents and teachers want them to do. When they sacrifice that leisure time, they "die" to it so they can devote that time to study.

If you're serious about physical fitness, you have to "die" to certain foods so you can eat the ones that are best for your health. The health and energy you gain is much superior to what you would get if you kept eating the wrong kinds of food.

So if you're used to making small sacrifices like that every day, why use such a stark word like "die"? Devoting yourself completely means to completely sever your connection with what you were like before. It evokes the phrase in the traditional wedding vow, "till death do us part," that signifies a relationship so intertwined that death is the only way it can be broken. You're so intertwined with your current condition that dying to your current life is the only way to make a break. And devoting yourself completely is how you can make that break.

Your words and actions demonstrate how thoroughly you've internalized what you've learned because it shows a new orientation, no longer a citizen of this world even though you still live and function in it. It's another reason why the image of crucifixion is so effective in helping you understand the completeness of devotion. A crucified person can only look in one direction: forward. On that cross, you can't look behind. And a crucified person is suspended between heaven and earth, not quite in heaven but certainly no longer of the earth.

When you devote yourself completely, it's like being put on display because sometimes, even family and friends won't understand why you chose some things over others. It may not be extreme like the persecution Christians experience in other countries where Christianity isn't tolerated, but you'll be noticed. In fact, you won't have to say much because your choices will probably speak for themselves.

But being put on display isn't the personal exhibition you see on reality television shows where people parade themselves for a short period of fame or notoriety. It's a function of recalling what God has done to remind yourself and others about the yawning gap between God and people which He has closed. Ancient Israel was commanded to do things like make sacrifices and bring offerings to remind them of the source of their hope and keep them focused on their unfinished business —

seeking God by remembering His attributes, the nature of His power, His deeds, and His example as well as being the channel through which God would bless other nations.

Devoting yourself completely is the final step that turns knowledge into habit. It's not an easy thing to get through, but the result is a set of habits that make you more likely to turn your faith and knowledge of what to do about it into action in more and more areas of your life. It's also forward progress that helps you carry on when your emotions say stop and keep seeking God when others tell you He's not to be found. To borrow Douglas MacArthur's words from his famous "Duty, Honor, Country" speech, you're continuing to love when love seems to fail, exercising faith when there seems to be little cause for faith, and creating hope when hope becomes forlorn.

John the Baptist settled his followers' concerns after they reported Jesus' growing popularity, explaining, "He must increase, but I must decrease" (John 3:30). Like John, you can actually increase in the four dimensions of life by stepping back, letting Jesus increase in your life. This last step of UPWARD will launch you on your next cycle of development as you continue to pursue the unfinished business God has presented you as His friend. You'll be presented with new opportunities to increase in the four dimensions of your life that help you see even more from God's perspective, and you'll bear greater fruit as you continue to learn how to be His blessing to others.

8

CONCLUSION: BEING AND BECOMING

Pursuing your unfinished business is a state of being and becoming. It's a state of "being" because while God is developing you into the friend He wants you to be, He looks at you as if you already achieved the expectations He has for you, a state made possible because He looks at you through the sacrifice Jesus Christ made to transform you into God's friend. But it's also a state of "becoming": while God looks at you as if you were already the friend He wants you to be, He also sets you on a path to become the kind of friend He knows you can be.

That sounds contradictory until you think about it in everyday terms. Ask what we call people who stand in front of a class and present lessons to students and you'll be told they're school teachers. And students, parents, and staff will confirm it, regarding them as school teachers even if they just graduated from college. But they're also on a path of continuing development, taking additional courses and attending training to achieve all that's expected of school teachers. In other words, they take that additional training because they're still becoming the kind of teachers they're expected to be.

The famous parable of the Prodigal Son tells about a young man who demanded his share of his inheritance and then squandered it until he was reduced to envying the hogs their slop. But when that son returned home broken by his experience, it was obvious he had changed, becoming the dutiful son his father dreamed he would be. Yet the father's reaction, an emotional and celebratory welcome, shows he never stopped viewing his son as worthy of love and high regard.

So the pressure to perform is off. Because you're in a state of "being," God regarding you already as having achieved everything He wants you to be, you have nothing left to prove.

Instead, you can concentrate on "becoming," pursuing your unfinished business in ways that integrate your faith into your daily life and turn you into an effective steward of your circumstances.

- Because pursuing your unfinished business makes you a steward of your circumstances, it requires you to know what to do about your friendship with God.

- You do this by making His priorities your priorities, a process of learning to see from God's perspective that turns your doubts into hope because the faith that makes you God's friend helps you see past your current circumstances to the potential He has in mind for you.

- But knowing what to do about that knowledge also gives you a burden to do something that can fulfill that hope. And doing something about it means becoming a servant.

So because pursuing your unfinished business is a journey of turning faith into the knowledge that builds hope and turning that knowledge into a servant's actions that are the evidence of love, it integrates those three great virtues, faith, hope, and love, into your everyday life. So delight not in your circumstances but in pursuing the unfinished business God has set before you.

ABOUT THE AUTHOR

Leroy Hurt has written and spoken about the practical challenge of turning one's faith into action, always the central question throughout a management and consulting career in the public and private sectors as well as service in local churches and non-profit organizations.

Educated at West Point, the University of Washington, and Regis University, he now lives in Olympia, Washington with his wife, Cathy.

www.YourUnfinishedBusiness.net